RISOTTOS, PAELLAS AND OTHER RICE SPECIALTIES

Raquel B. Agranoff

BRISTOL PUBLISHING ENTERPRISES
San Leandro, California

a nitty gritty® cookbook

ISBN 1-55867-166-8

Cover design: Frank J. Paredes
Cover photography: John A. Benson
Food stylist: Susan Massey
Illustrator: James Balkovek

CONTENTS

This is for Will and Adam, great sons and knowledgeable critics.

Sincere thanks for their invaluable recipe testing go to MariCarmen Davies, Vivian Garcia-Ribiero, Annie Gonzales, Anna Greeven, Florence Kandiner, Patricia Korten, Lucille Ragland, Kathyrn Starkey, Donna K. Tope, Charlotte VanCurler and Lilibeth Warner.

ABOUT THE RICES IN THIS BOOK

FACTS AND FANTASIES

Long-grain, short-grain, brown, polished, red, purple, sweet, sticky —any way you look at it, rice supplies over half the world's population with sustenance. Rituals and religions have sprung from rice, and are integrated into almost every culture that uses it. Much of the lore has to do with power and fertility. From the time it was first cultivated in northern Thailand, and as it spread to China and India, and on to the rest of the world, rice has gathered all those who have grown it, eaten it, and experimented with it into its bountiful arms. In China, as far back as 3000 years ago, the emperor himself planted the first and best seeds each year. This honor was then passed on to other members of the family, who finished planting the rest of the seeds. Even today in some parts of China, to inquire after one's health is implicit in the greeting, "Have you eaten your rice today?"

Almost every culture that uses rice sees it as a meaningful symbol. For instance, Greeks sometimes put rice in the shoes of the bride to assure her fertility. Arabs, who call rice *aish*, meaning *life*, place grains of rice on the roof of the house to prevent misfortune from raining down upon the family therein. In China, a greeting for the new year may be "May your rice never burn," and to upset one's rice bowl is a sign of bad luck. Children are coaxed into eating every grain of rice in their bowls with the admonition that for every grain left, their future mate will have a pock mark!

In ancient times a Dragon Boat Festival was held in central China to ceremonialize and mark the ritual of the transplanting of rice. This is the time when the rice seedlings are moved to their final growing place. The ritual was usually held in late spring and portrayed the activities of dead ancestors who traveled by dragon boat to the land of the living. This ritual is thought to be a precursor of the great dragon parades still seen during the Chinese New Year. In the time of Confucius, a sacrificial bowl of rice had to be of the highest quality, carefully grown and stored so that no fermentation had taken place. His meal was to be mainly rice, so that when he spoke to the gods his breath would be sweetly scented.

The Japanese currently hold similar festivals during the transplanting season, in some areas asking the blessings of Shinto priests. Believing in the mystical powers of rice is not restricted to a time or place in history. Even Rembrandt is said to have preceded the start of a new painting now and then by having a bowl of steamed rice.

A FEW VARIETIES

There are over 40,000 varieties of rice. Each population region is devoted to its own variety, cultivated in its own area. During the Korean War, for example, soldiers from the Philippines would eat only their native rice, which had to be flown in. Once you are aware that rices are very distinct from one another, the differences become very apparent. Although there may not be much difference in their caloric content, there are important differences as to how each of the basic sizes of rice absorbs liquid, and this is directly related to how each type is best prepared and used.

White rice is preferred to brown rice by many, but if rice is the major food source, as it often is in underdeveloped regions of the world, loss of the bran coating that is present in brown rice can lead to a serious vitamin deficiency.

Long-grain rice, which is about four times as long as it is wide, when properly cooked separates, and becomes somewhat fluffy. This makes it perfect for salads and pilafs.

- *Basmati* or *Texmati rice* is a long-grain, aromatic, nutty-flavored white or brown rice usually imported from India or Pakistan, but now grown in the United States.

- *Brown rice* is commonly a long-grain, whole-grain rice that still has its brown, high-fiber bran coating. Brown rice has a nutty flavor, provides greater nutrition than white rice and takes longer to cook.

Medium-grain rice is slightly plumper and stickier than long-grain rice, making it cling together. This makes it seem creamier, and ideal for desserts such as rice pudding. There are wonderful new medium-grain rices being grown in California now, such as Kokuho and Nishiki.

Short-grain rice, which is almost rounded in appearance, has a higher starch content than other rices, and the grains tend to stick together.

- Sometimes short-grain rices are called *pearl* or *round* rice.
- *Glutinous rice* is a short-grain rice, also known as sticky, waxy or sweet rice. It is most often used in Asian sweets and snacks. It is not an everyday table rice.
- *Arborio* is a very special type of short-grain rice, which, having a high starch content, is able to absorb large quantities of liquid. In this book, when preparing risotto, we use Arborio. The desired end product is meant to have both a creamy consistency and a firm center to each grain. In addition, the cooking method, which consists of adding hot liquid a little at a time, permits the rice to absorb almost three times its volume in liquid. That liquid can be beef, fish, vegetable, duck or chicken stock, sometimes mixed with wine. The Po Valley is the cradle of rice culture in Italy, although rice is grown in other areas, including Tuscany, Calabria and Sicily. *Nano, Carnarole* and *Vialone* are a few other types of rice from Italy that are also suitable for making risotto. *Granza* rice from Spain, although used mostly for cooking paellas, can also be used to make risotto. Italian rice for risotto can also be grouped according to size and preference of region. The four sizes are called *comune* (smallest) or *originario, semifino, fino* and *superfino* (largest grain). Arborio rice is readily

available in many supermarkets or specialty stores. Superfino is the best size for making risotto.

STORAGE

Rice should be stored in a cool, dry place in a covered container. White rice is the least perishable, and will keep indefinitely. This is not true for brown, glutinous and aromatic rices, whose shelf life is about 6 months. If you have room in your refrigerator, the shelf life of these more perishable rices will be extended by a few months.

BASICS

HOW TO RECONSTITUTE DRIED MUSHROOMS

Place dried mushrooms in a small saucepan with water to cover. Bring to a boil, reduce heat and simmer for 5 minutes. Turn off heat and let mushrooms soak for 30 minutes. Drain through cheesecloth, reserving liquid. Rinse mushrooms and drain again. Spread mushrooms on paper towels, wipe off any foreign bits of matter or dirt, and rinse again. Strain reserved liquid from first soaking through a very fine strainer or paper coffee filter. Freeze or store unused liquid in the refrigerator to flavor other dishes.

COOKING WITH HERBS

When fresh herbs are paired with dried herbs of the same type, a more intense flavor is the result than using either one by itself. For example: fresh lemon thyme combined with dried thyme or fresh sage with dried, rubbed sage. When cooking with herbs, remember to use dried herbs sparingly, and be lavish with fresh herbs.

HOW TO PEEL AND SEED A TOMATO

Blanch a tomato: Dip it in boiling water for 10 to 30 seconds. Plunge it into cold water, and the skin will be easy to peel. Cut in half and squeeze out seeds. To dice, remove inner membranes and flatten tomato halves. Cut into strips and dice.

HOW TO TOAST NUTS

Heat oven to 375°. Place nuts on a piece of parchment paper, waxed paper or aluminum foil on a baking sheet and toast in oven for 5 to 8 minutes. Check after 3 minutes, and shake pan to turn nuts over. When nuts become slightly darker, remove them from the oven. If you have used nuts which still have their skin, turn them out onto a clean dishtowel and rub them briskly together. The skins should rub off easily. The toasted flavor of the nuts will enhance any recipe.

HOW TO ROAST AND PEEL PEPPERS

For a gas stove: Turn gas burner to high and place the whole pepper directly into the flame. The skin will become black and charred. Turn pepper frequently, using long tongs and an oven glove. When pepper is completely black, remove from flame and place immediately in a paper or plastic bag. Be careful to wait until any sparks that may appear on the pepper (especially the stem) are extinguished. As you become more adept, you may be able to do 2 or 3 peppers at a time. Peppers will steam inside the bag, making the charred skins easy to remove. Steam for about 10 minutes. Rub off skins under running water, and place skinned peppers in a colander to drain. Remove stems, ribs and seeds from each pepper. If you are not using peppers immediately, store in the refrigerator in a sealed container.

For an electric stove: Heat the broiler. Cut in peppers in half, remove seeds and stem, and press down to flatten. Trim off ribs with a sharp paring knife and discard. Place peppers skin-side up on a baking sheet under broiler. Skins will eventually become charred. Steam and rub off skins as in gas stove directions. You can also roast peppers on a grill following these directions.

HOW TO TOAST AND GRIND SEEDS

Grinding whole toasted spice seeds releases essential oils and produces a heady aroma and flavor. To toast seeds, spread about 3 tbs. in a small dry sauté pan. Place over medium heat and toast until seeds are light brown. Shake pan to keep seeds from burning. Grind cooled seeds with a food processor, spice grinder, blender, or mortar and pestle. Store leftover ground seeds in a tightly covered container.

HOW TO TOAST COCONUT

Heat oven to 350°. Spread coconut in a shallow pan and bake, stirring occasionally, until lightly toasted, about 12 to 15 minutes.

HOW TO COOK RICE

In all cases, these examples call for 1 cup uncooked rice. Use a 2- to 3-quart pot with a lid and add 1 tsp. salt.

Long-grain white rice: Combine rice and salt with 2 cups liquid, bring to a boil, reduce heat and cook covered over low heat for 15 to 20 minutes. Remove from heat and leave covered for 10 minutes. Yield: 3 cups.

Basmati or Texmati rice: Combine rice and salt with $1\frac{1}{2}$ to 2 cups liquid. Bring to a boil, reduce heat and cook covered over low heat for about 15 minutes. Remove from heat and leave covered for 5 minutes. Yield: about 3 cups.

Brown rice: Combine rice and salt with $2\frac{1}{2}$ cups liquid, bring to a boil, reduce heat and cook covered over low heat for 45 to 50 minutes. Yield: 3-4 cups.

Short- or medium-grain white rice: Combine rice and salt with $1\frac{3}{4}$ cups liquid, bring to a boil, reduce heat and cook covered over low heat for 15 to 20 minutes. Do not remove cover. Remove from heat and leave cover on for 10 minutes. Yield: 3 cups.

Glutinous rice: Wash in several changes of water before using to remove any cornstarch, which is usually added to keep the grains separate. Combine rice and salt with $1\frac{1}{2}$ cups liquid and bring to a boil. Reduce heat and cook covered for 15 to 20 minutes. Yield: about 2 cups.

Arborio rice: Find complete cooking instructions on pages 13 to 23.

OTHER COOKING METHODS FOR RICE

Boiling water method: You can cook rice in boiling water in the same way you cook pasta. Boil 2 to 3 quarts water in a large pot and toss in 1 to 2 cups rice and 1 tsp. salt. Bring to a rolling boil and watch closely. In about 20 to 25 minutes, rice will be done. Drain well. Yield: about 3-4 cups.

Oven method: Sauté ½ chopped onion in about 1 to 2 tbs. butter or olive oil. Add 1 cup white rice, turning to coat all grains. Transfer rice mixture to a 1½-quart ovenproof dish and add 2 cups boiling stock and 1 tsp. salt. Cover with a tight-fitting lid, and place in 350° oven. Increase stock to 2½ cups for brown rice. Cook for 20 minutes for white rice and up to 40 minutes for brown rice. Yield: 3 cups white rice; 3½ cups brown rice.

STORING AND REHEATING COOKED RICE

Cooked rice can be refrigerated for a few days, or even frozen. Thaw before reheating, so the grains will separate properly. Reheat on the stove or in the microwave. Add a little liquid, about 3 tbs. for 2 cups of cooked rice, and reheat in a shallow pan to maintain control of the process so that the bottom grains do not get gummy while the top ones remain unheated. If you reheat in the microwave, cover the dish and heat on HIGH for about 1½ minutes per cup of cooked rice.

SOURCES FOR SPECIAL RICES

ZINGERMAN'S
Catalog Department
422 Detroit Street
Ann Arbor, MI 48104
313-769-1625
zing @ chamber.ann-arbor.mi.us

DEAN AND DELUCA
560 Broadway
New York, NY 10021
800-221-7714

SUTTON PLACE GOURMET
3201 New Mexico Ave., N.W.
Washington, DC 20016
202-363-5800

MERCHANT CELLAR COLLECTION
254 W. Maple
Birmingham, MI 48009
810-433-3000

G.B. RATTO, INTERNATIONAL GROCERS
821 Washington St.
Oakland, CA 94607
510-832-6503

UNDERSTANDING AND COOKING RISOTTO

UNDERSTANDING AND COOKING RISOTTO

Cooking risotto is different from cooking any other type of long- or short-grain white rice. *Arborio* rice from Italy, (or *Granza* rice from Spain) has a very high starch content, which makes it an ideal medium for absorbing liquid and producing creamy risotto. The United States also produces Arborio rice.

Basically, butter or oil is heated and minced onions are added and cooked until soft. Rice is added to this mixture and coated with the cooking fat. When the center of the grain turns white, small amounts of hot stock, sometimes combined with wine, are added in increments as the mixture is constantly stirred. As each amount of stock is absorbed by the rice, more is added. When the rice becomes tender on the outside of the grain, but still slightly firm in the center (a state referred to as *al dente*, or "to the tooth"), the cooking is stopped. The quantity of liquid added is not exact. Salt, butter and grated fresh Reggiano Parmesan cheese are mixed in. Sometimes saffron threads, crushed and steeped in stock, are added.

Although risotto is often served as a first course, many of the risotto recipes here are suggested as entrées. Risotto can be made the conventional way, on top of the stove, or with a pressure cooker, microwave or rice cooker. Here basic recipes act as guidelines, but you should always follow the manufacturers' instructions for your appliance.

STOCKS FOR RISOTTO: VEGETABLE STOCK

Vegetable stock adds a bright, fresh flavor to many recipes, and is the choice for vegetarian rice dishes.

2 medium onions, coarsely chopped
1 leek, cleaned and coarsely chopped
2 medium carrots, coarsely chopped
4 celery stalks, including leaves,
    coarsely chopped
1 medium tomato, quartered

2-3 sprigs flat-leaf parsley
1 small turnip, quartered
1 tsp. salt
4-5 peppercorns
3-4 bay leaves, crumbled
3 qt. water

Place all ingredients in a heavy 4- or 5-quart pot. Bring to a boil, cover with a lid slightly askew, lower heat and simmer for 1½ to 2 hours. Check liquid occasionally, and add more water to maintain about 3 quarts stock. Cool and strain stock through cheesecloth over a strainer. Taste for seasons and adjust if necessary. Discard cooked vegetables. Store in the refrigerator or freezer.

STOCKS FOR RISOTTO: FISH STOCK

Yield: about 10 cups

You can use any chopped vegetables in addition to those in the recipe. A fennel bulb is a flavorful addition. This stock freezes very well. Freeze it in 2- or 3-cup amounts, so you can also have it available for sauces. Use trimmings from mild-flavored white fish.

2 lb. fish trimmings (heads, bones)
1 medium onion, peeled and cut into chunks
1-2 stalks celery, chopped
3 bay leaves
4-5 peppercorns
½ tsp. salt
1 cup dry white wine
water to cover

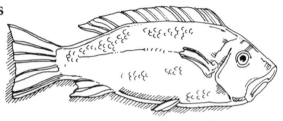

Fill a heavy 4- or 5-quart pot with all ingredients. Bring to a boil, turn down heat and simmer for about 30 to 45 minutes. Skim off and discard any foam that rises to the top of simmering stock. Cool and strain stock through cheesecloth over a strainer. Store for 1 to 2 days in the refrigerator.

STOCKS FOR RISOTTO: CHICKEN OR TURKEY STOCK

Yield: about 10 cups

If you prefer a darker stock, brown the chicken parts and vegetables in a 400° oven before proceeding with the recipe. You can also include the bones and meat from cooked poultry, but remember that the flavorings you used to make the initial cooking will accent the final stock.

3-4 lb. chicken pieces (backs, necks or
    trimmings)
water to cover
2-3 carrots
3 stalks celery with leaves, cut into chunks
1-2 onions, outer peel removed,
    quartered

turnips, tomatoes, cleaned leeks or
    parsnips, chopped, optional
6 whole peppercorns
1 tbs. salt
2-3 bay leaves
2-3 sprigs fresh thyme
2-3 sprigs fresh rosemary

Place chicken pieces in a heavy 5-quart pot and cover with water. Add vegetables. Bring to a boil and add peppercorns, salt and bay leaves. Turn heat down to simmer and cook for 2 hours. Add fresh thyme and rosemary about 30 minutes before stock is done. Skim off and discard any foam that rises to the surface. Strain stock through a sieve. Cool stock to room temperature and refrigerate overnight. Remove fat from top of stock and freeze if not using within 1 to 2 days.

STOCKS FOR RISOTTO: BEEF STOCK

Yield: about 10 cups

Browning the meat and bones will give the finished stock an appetizing color.

2-3 lb. boneless beef chuck
1-2 beef soup bones
1 tbs. vegetable oil
2-3 carrots, cut into chunks
2-3 stalks celery with leaves, cut into
   chunks
1 cup chopped leeks
½ cup chopped fresh flat-leaf parsley

2 medium onions, outer skin removed,
   halved
6 whole peppercorns
3-4 bay leaves
1 tbs. salt
1 tomato, halved
water to cover

Place beef and beef bones in a heavy 4-quart pot with vegetable oil. Brown meat and bones on all sides over high heat. Turn off heat and add carrots, celery and leaves, chopped leeks, parsley, onions, peppercorns, bay leaves, salt and tomato. Cover with water and bring to a boil. Reduce heat to simmer, and cook for 3 hours, or until meat is soft. Skim off and discard foam that rises to the surface. If water evaporates too quickly, place a lid on top of the pot, leaving pot slightly uncovered. When stock is cooked, strain through a sieve, reserving meat for another use. Cool to room temperature, and refrigerate overnight. Remove fat from top of stock. If not using within 1 to 2 days, store in a freezer.

STOCKS FOR RISOTTO: DUCK STOCK

Yield: 10-12 cups

If you reserve the duck fat when you are through, you will find it very good for sautéing potatoes.

uncooked wing tips, neck and giblets from a duck
leftover bones from a cooked duck, optional
3 qt. water
2 cups chopped combined celery, carrots and onion
1 bay leaf
1/2 tsp. salt
1/4 tsp. freshly ground pepper
3 juniper berries, crushed

In a heavy 4-quart pot, cover duck pieces with water. Add chopped vegetables, bay leaf, salt, pepper and juniper berries. Bring to a boil, turn down heat and simmer for about 2 hours. Skim off and discard any foam that rises to the surface. Strain stock through a sieve and discard vegetables. Cool stock to room temperature, chill in the refrigerator and remove fat from top of stock. If not using within 5 days, store in a freezer.

BASIC RISOTTO

Yield: about 5½ cups

A bowl of freshly made risotto, laced with grated Reggiano Parmesan cheese, is a dish fit for the most discerning palate. Accompany it with your favorite spinach salad, some crusty bread and fresh fruit tarts for dessert. Or serve it as a first course, with something like poached salmon. Choose the stock that complements your meal. Replace 1 cup of the stock with 1 cup dry white wine, if desired.

3 tbs. butter or olive oil, or a mixture
½ cup diced onion
2 cups Arborio rice
1 tsp. salt
6-7 cups simmering stock (see pages 15-19)

1 cup dry white wine to replace 1 cup stock, optional
½ cup grated Reggiano Parmesan cheese
1 tbs. butter

Heat butter or olive oil in a 3-quart pot. Sauté minced onion until soft. Add rice, and using a wooden spoon, turn frequently until all grains are coated with oil. Add salt. Continue to stir rice while it is cooking. Add hot stock 1 cup at a time. As each cup of stock is absorbed, add more. Save about ½ cup stock to add just before serving. In about 20 minutes, rice grains should be *al dente*, with a soft outside, but a firm center. Add 1 tbs. butter, reserved ½ cup stock and Parmesan. Taste for seasoning and add salt if desired. If you are using the risotto in another recipe, omit cheese.

RICE COOKER RISOTTO

Be sure to follow the manufacturers' directions for your rice cooker. You will generally use less stock than this recipe calls for.

4 tbs. butter or olive oil
1/2 cup diced onion
2 cups Arborio rice
1/2 cup dry white wine to replace 1/2 cup stock, optional
3-4 cups simmering stock (see pages 15-19)
1 tsp. salt
1/2 cup grated Reggiano Parmesan cheese

Turn on the rice cooker and melt 3 tbs. butter. When butter is hot, add diced onion, sautéing until soft. Add rice, turning to coat all grains with fat. Pour in stock, measuring the amount needed to make rice on the "hard" side. Add salt. Cover and cook until the machine shuts off. Be careful not to let rice sit too long, as it most certainly will get soft. Remove lid and add remaining butter and grated cheese. If you are using the risotto in another recipe, omit cheese and remove risotto from rice cooker.

PRESSURE COOKER RISOTTO

Yield: about 5 cups

The advantage of using a pressure cooker is that it eliminates the necessity of stirring. You will have to practice a bit with your pressure cooker to determine the exact length of cooking time, as there may be differences in various cookers needed to produce an al dente risotto, but here is one that works for me. Again, be familiar with manufacturers' directions.

2 tbs. olive oil
1 tbs. butter
½ cup diced onion
2 cups Arborio rice

1 tsp. salt
4 cups simmering stock (see pages 15-19)
½ cup dry white wine, optional
½ cup grated Reggiano Parmesan cheese

Heat butter and oil in an uncovered pressure cooker. Add onion and cook until soft. Add rice and mix with a wooden spoon to coat all grains with fat. Add salt, stock and white wine, if using, and cover. Bring cooker to high pressure. Cook at high pressure for about 11 minutes. Bring pressure down and remove cover. If liquid is not entirely absorbed, place pot over high heat for 1 to 2 minutes, stirring constantly. Stir in cheese, or, if you are using the risotto in another recipe, omit cheese.

MICROWAVE RISOTTO

Yield: about 5 cups

The advantage of cooking risotto in a microwave is that it requires less stirring. Starch absorbs liquid slowly and completely in a microwave oven. This means that the stock is slowly absorbed, leaving the rice slightly firm. Use an 8- to 10-cup microwave baking dish, about 2 or 3 inches deep.

3 tbs. butter
1 tbs. vegetable oil
¾ cup diced onion
2 cups Arborio rice
5 cups stock, room temperature (see
    pages 15-19)

½ cup dry white wine, optional
1 tsp. salt
½ cup grated Reggiano Parmesan cheese

Heat butter and oil in a microwave baking dish for about 2 minutes over high heat. Lower heat to medium, add onions and cover. Cook for 3 minutes. Add rice, stirring to coat all grains with fat. Cook, uncovered, for 3 minutes. Add stock, white wine, if using, and salt and cook uncovered for about 8 minutes. Stir and cook for another 8 to 10 minutes. Taste for seasoning and add more salt if necesssary. Stir in cheese, or, if you are using the risotto in another recipe, omit cheese.

RISOTTOS

SHRIMP AND PORK RISOTTO WITH BLACK BEANS

Ground pork and shrimp are cooked with Italian Arborio rice and Asian fermented black beans. This is truly a cross-ethnic delight! Fermented black beans are sometimes called "salty black beans," and are a Chinese specialty.

3 tbs. fermented black beans
3 cloves garlic, minced or pressed
1/4 cup soy sauce
2 tbs. vegetable oil
1/4 lb. ground pork
1 1/2 lb. large shrimp (size 26-30 per lb.), peeled and deveined
1/2 cup vegetable stock (see page 15)
2 eggs, beaten
2 tbs. vegetable oil
1/2 cup minced shallots
2 cloves garlic, minced, optional
1 1/2 cups Arborio rice
5 cups simmering vegetable stock (see page 15)
chopped scallions for garnish

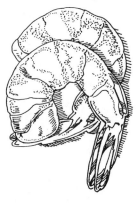

Rinse fermented black beans to remove some of the salt. Place beans, 3 cloves garlic and soy sauce in a small bowl, pressing down on beans with the back of a spoon to soften. Set aside. Heat 2 tbs. vegetable oil in a large sauté pan over medium heat and cook pork until no longer pink. Add shrimp and cook very briefly until slightly undercooked and not translucent. Add bean mixture, $1/2$ cup vegetable stock and beaten eggs. Remove pan from heat and set aside.

Heat 2 tbs. vegetable oil in a 3-quart pot over medium heat and sauté shallots and 2 cloves garlic, if using. Add Arborio rice and stir to coat all grains with fat. Add hot stock, 1 cup at a time. Keep stirring contents of pot, and when rice has absorbed liquid, add more stock. When rice is almost finished cooking, in about 12 to 14 minutes, add pork and shrimp mixture. Add more hot stock, continuing to stir and cook until grains of rice are slightly hard in the center and tender on the outside, *al dente*. Serve hot, sprinkled with scallions, on individual plates.

SQUASH, SAGE AND GINGER RISOTTO

Servings: 4 as first course

Acorn, hubbard or any winter squash combines with fresh sage and ginger, resulting in a risotto that is savory and aromatic. Cooking it in a pressure cooker means this is a dish that can be prepared in 30 minutes. Double the ingredients for a main course for 6. Dried and fresh sage used together boost the flavor.

1 tbs. olive oil
2 tbs. butter
½ cup minced onion
3 cloves garlic, minced
1 tsp. dried sage
1 cup diced acorn squash
1 tbs. minced ginger root

1 cup Arborio rice
2⅔ cups simmering chicken stock (see page 17)
½ tsp. salt
1 cup grated Reggiano Parmesan cheese
2 tbs. chopped fresh sage

Heat olive oil and butter in an uncovered pressure cooker over medium heat. Add onion and garlic and sauté until soft. Mix in dried sage. Add squash and ginger. Cook for a few minutes. Add rice and stir to coat all grains with oil. Add chicken stock and place lid on pressure cooker. Cook at high pressure for about 12 minutes. Remove from heat, reduce pressure and remove lid. Add ¾ cup of the Parmesan cheese and fresh sage; mix well. Spoon risotto into warm bowls. Pass remaining cheese.

RUBY RISOTTO

Servings: 6

For those of us who view a day without carbohydrates as a day without the sun, this recipe is truly a gem. It had never occurred to me that risotto could be made with red wine until I tasted it, but it makes perfect gastronomic sense. If white wine, why not red? I think that the extra dimension of taste that is added is superb. Judge for yourself.

½ sweet onion, diced
3 tbs. butter or olive oil
2 cups Arborio rice
1 cup dry red wine

5-6 cups simmering chicken stock (see page 17)
1 cup grated Reggiano Parmesan cheese
freshly ground pepper to taste
½ tsp. salt, optional

In a large sauté pan, sauté onion in butter over medium heat until soft. Add rice and mix until all grains have been coated with butter. Add red wine and stir briefly. Add hot chicken stock about 1 cup at a time. As each cup of stock is absorbed, add the next cup, stirring constantly. When rice is *al dente*, add ¾ cup of the Parmesan cheese. Add pepper and salt, if using. Serve with remaining cheese.

VARIATION
Add 1 cup chopped radicchio, which has been sautéed briefly in butter.

RISOTTO CARBONNADE

The term "carbonnade a la flamande" refers to a thick Belgian stew made with bacon, beef, beer and sugar, among other ingredients. In this recipe, beer is substituted for some of the usual stock in making the risotto. Admittedly, it is a little unorthodox, but the taste is addictive.

2 tbs. butter
1 tbs. olive oil
8 oz. fresh mushrooms
6 oz. lean bacon, cut into ½-inch dice
1 lb. stewing beef, cut into 1-inch pieces
2 tbs. brown sugar
1-2 tbs. olive oil, optional
1 cup minced onions
1 cup minced carrots
2 cloves garlic, minced, or more to taste
2 cups Arborio rice
3 cups simmering beef stock (see page 18) mixed with 2 cups beer
½ cup chopped fresh flat-leaf parsley
salt and pepper to taste

Keep beef stock-beer mixture hot. In a 4-quart saucepan, melt butter with olive oil and add fresh mushrooms. Cook over high heat for 2 or 3 minutes. Remove mushrooms and add diced bacon. Lower heat to medium and sauté bacon until brown and cooked through. Remove bacon and add stewing beef. When beef is brown and thoroughly cooked, add brown sugar and cook briefly. Remove beef from pot and add olive oil, if pot is dry. Sauté minced onions and carrots until soft, but not brown. Add garlic and cook for 1 minute. Add Arborio rice and turn to coat grains with fat. Add beef stock-beer mixture in 1-cup increments. As each cup is absorbed, add more liquid, stirring constantly. When grains are still slightly firm at the center, and soft on the outside, *al dente*, return bacon, beef and mushrooms to pot. Mix to incorporate ingredients evenly. Add parsley, salt and pepper. Taste and adjust seasonings, if necessary.

SAUSAGE, APRICOT AND RAISIN RISOTTO

Servings: 6

One of the attributes of risotto is that it merges well with many ingredients. It provides contrast when there may be spiciness, and creaminess when combined with something crunchy. It always makes any dish greater than the sum of its parts. Here is a perfect example that combines dried fruits with fennel sausage and risotto, and comes up with a delectable main course.

1 tbs. olive oil
8 oz. fennel sausage, casings removed
1/2 medium onion, sliced
1 clove garlic, minced
1 tsp. red pepper flakes
1 1/2 cups coarsely chopped snow peas
2 tbs. olive oil
1/2 cup chopped onion
1/4 cup chopped carrot

1 tsp. dried oregano
2 cups Arborio rice
6-7 cups simmering beef or chicken
    stock (see pages 18, 17)
3/4 cup coarsely chopped dried apricots
1/2 cup raisins
3 tbs. chopped fresh oregano
salt and pepper to taste
1 cup grated Reggiano Parmesan cheese

Heat 1 tbs. olive oil in a large sauté pan over medium-high heat. Cook sausage until no longer pink. Remove sausage and sauté sliced onion and garlic until wilted. Add red pepper flakes and return sausage to pan. Cook for 1 minute to blend flavors. Add chopped snow peas and cook for 1 minute. Remove pan from heat and set aside.

Heat 2 tbs. olive oil in a 3-quart pot over medium heat. Add onion, carrot and dried oregano. Stir and cook until vegetables are soft. Add Arborio rice and stir to coat all grains with oil. Add hot stock, 1 cup at a time, stirring constantly. As liquid is absorbed, add the next cup. After 10 minutes, add chopped apricots and raisins. Continue to cook. When rice is *al dente*, or still slightly firm in the center of each grain and soft on the outside, add chopped fresh oregano, sausage mixture, salt, pepper and Parmesan cheese. Mix well and serve hot in warm individual bowls.

RISOTTO MILANESE

No risotto cookbook would be complete without including the classic Risotto alla Milanese. Because we are making this in a pressure cooker, the cooking time is reduced to 11 or 12 minutes, rather than 20 or more. Moreover, the necessity of constant stirring is eliminated. Because this is such a simple recipe, with few components, it is important to use the best ingredients available. Unsalted fresh butter, Arborio rice, saffron and a full-flavored homemade stock will produce a sublime risotto.

6-8 saffron threads, or ¼ tsp. saffron powder
6 cups simmering beef or chicken stock (see page 18, 17)
¼ cup butter
¾ cup minced onion
2 cups Arborio rice
1 cup dry white wine
1 tbs. butter
1 cup grated Reggiano Parmesan cheese

Soak saffron threads or powder in ½ cup of stock and set aside. Melt butter in an uncovered pressure cooker over medium heat and add minced onion. Cook until onion is soft. Add Arborio rice and stir until all grains are coated with butter. Add white wine and cook for 3 to 4 minutes. Add all of the remaining hot stock and place lid on cooker. Bring to high pressure and cook for 11 to 12 minutes. Remove from heat, reduce pressure, remove lid and add saffron and stock. Stir well and add 1 tbs. butter and grated Parmesan cheese. Spoon into warm individual serving bowls.

RISOTTO WITH BRAISED DUCK AND SHIITAKE MUSHROOMS

Servings: 6

If you don't happen to have leftover braised duck on hand — you don't?! —, this is still a fairly easy recipe. You can substitute chicken or turkey for the duck. It's the braising technique that is important. The duck is browned first, and then braised in the oven with vegetables and green olives. The shiitake mushrooms are a succulent component of this dish.

1 Long Island duckling, about 5 lb.
salt
2 tbs. vegetable oil
2 carrots, peeled
1 medium onion, chopped
2 cloves garlic, minced
1 tbs. dried thyme
1 cup chicken or duck stock (see page 17, 19)
1 cup unpitted imported green olives
5-6 large dried shiitake mushrooms, reconstituted (see page 7)
2 tbs. grated ginger root

1 clove garlic, minced
1 tbs. soy sauce
4 cups chicken or duck stock
1 tbs. vegetable oil
1 tbs. butter
2 leeks, white part only, cleaned and sliced
1 cup diced turnips, optional
2 cups Arborio rice
¼ tsp. salt
freshly ground pepper to taste
¾ cup grated Reggiano Parmesan cheese

Heat oven to 400°. Snip wing tips from duck. Rinse duck, wipe dry and sprinkle with salt inside and out. Heat 2 tbs. vegetable oil in a large heavy Dutch oven with a lid. Brown duck on all sides over high heat. Remove from pot, reduce heat to medium, and sauté carrots, onion and 2 cloves garlic until soft. Add thyme and cook for 1 to 2 minutes. Add 1 cup stock. Return duck to pot, cover and place in oven. Braise, covered, for 45 minutes. Add olives to pot and braise for another 15 minutes. Slice mushrooms into thin strips and mix with ginger root, 1 clove garlic and soy sauce.

Cool braised duck and set aside cooked olives from pot. Remove meat from bones, reserving skin.* Shred or dice meat, measure 2 cups and set aside (reserve leftover meat for another use). Discard braising stock and vegetables.

Heat remaining stock to simmering. Heat 1 tbs. vegetable oil and butter in a 3-quart pot over medium-high heat and sauté sliced leeks until wilted. Add diced turnips, if using, and cook for 1 minute. Add Arborio rice and stir to coat all grains with fat. Add 1 cup of the hot stock and continue to stir over high heat. As rice absorbs liquid, add more liquid, and stir constantly until rice is still slightly firm in the center and soft on the outside, *al dente*. Remove pot from heat and add salt and freshly ground pepper to taste. Gently fold in duck meat, braised olives and ½ cup of the grated Parmesan cheese. Serve in warm bowls; pass remaining grated cheese.

* The duck skin can be cut into 1-inch square pieces and browned in the oven. This is elegant sprinkled on a green salad and will enhance mashed potatoes in a fabulous way.

RISOTTO WITH PEPPERS AND MONKFISH

Servings: 6-8

Here is a colorful risotto with roasted red and yellow peppers, perfumed with saffron and thyme and studded with sautéed monkfish. It is both light and savory and has tremendous eye appeal. You can substitute cooked lobster or shrimp, or use a combination of all three. The importance of using a good fish stock cannot be overemphasized.

1½ lb. fresh monkfish, cut into bite-sized pieces
½ tsp. sweet paprika
1 tsp. cumin seeds, toasted and ground (see page 9)
1 clove garlic, minced
1 tsp. dried thyme
3 tbs. olive oil
¾ cup dry white wine
2 tbs. chopped fresh thyme
1-2 cups diced roasted yellow and red bell peppers (see page 8)

¼ tsp. salt
2 tbs. olive oil
2 tbs. butter
¾ cup minced onion
2 cups Arborio rice
¼ tsp. crushed saffron threads, soaked in ¼ cup stock
5½-6 cups simmering fish stock (see page 16)
salt and freshly ground pepper to taste

Marinate monkfish pieces for at least 30 minutes in paprika, cumin, garlic, dried thyme and 3 tbs. olive oil. While rice is cooking, or very shortly before, heat a large sauté pan. Add marinated monkfish a few pieces at a time and sauté over high heat for 4 to 5 minutes, or until fish is fully cooked. Do not add too many pieces at a time, or the fish will steam, rather than sauté, and become mushy. Fish should be firm. Do not overcook. Remove cooked fish from pan and place in a bowl. Add white wine to pan and cook over high heat until wine is reduced by half. Pour reduced wine over monkfish. Add fresh thyme, roasted peppers and salt to fish and set aside.

Heat 2 tbs. oil and butter in a 4-quart saucepan over medium heat. Add minced onion and cook until soft. Add Arborio rice and turn to coat all grains with oil. Add saffron and liquid; mix well. Add hot stock, 1 cup at a time, stirring constantly. As each cup is absorbed, add the next. Keep stirring. Rice will become plump as it soaks up the liquid. Continue to add hot stock until rice is cooked *al dente*, with a center somewhat firm and the outside soft. You may not have to use all of the liquid. Add cooked monkfish mixture. Taste for seasoning and add salt and pepper if necessary. Serve hot.

CREAMY RICE AND STILTON RISOTTO CASSEROLE

I must confess, casseroles are among my favorite comfort foods. This is a satisfying, tummy-hugging dish. It can be part of a delicious lunch when accompanied by a crisp salad and a light dessert, or, in smaller servings, as a first course for a formal dinner.

1½ cups chicken stock (see page 17)
1½ cups milk (can be low-fat)
12 oz. crumbled or diced Stilton cheese
2 tbs. butter or olive oil
¼ cup finely diced onion
2 cloves garlic, minced, or more to taste
1½ cups Arborio rice
¼ tsp. salt
1 cup coarsely chopped fresh snow peas
½ cup half-and-half
¼ tsp. freshly ground pepper
salt to taste
½ cup pine nuts, toasted (see page 8)

Heat oven to 350°. Combine chicken stock and milk in a small saucepan over medium heat. Add Stilton cheese, stirring to melt. Keep mixture warm while proceeding with recipe. Heat butter or olive oil in an ovenproof 2-quart saucepan over medium heat and sauté onion and garlic until soft, but not brown.

Add rice, stirring to coat all grains with oil. Add 1 cup of the warmed stock-milk mixture and salt. As liquid is absorbed, add another cup, stirring constantly. Keep stirring rice as it cooks. When second cup of liquid is absorbed, add remaining liquid. Cover pot with a tight-fitting lid and place in oven for 15 minutes. Remove lid (be careful of steam), and mix in snow peas, half-and-half, pepper and salt. Replace lid and place pot in oven for 5 minutes. Uncover pot and return to oven for 5 minutes. Sprinkle with toasted pine nuts and serve immediately.

CURRIED RISOTTO

Servings: 6

Risotto with curry and dried fruit may sound a little strange, but it is tasty and attractive. You can serve this as a vegetarian dish, or add 1 cup of flaked cooked or canned salmon. The creaminess of the risotto is enhanced by the unorthodox addition of mozzarella cheese and is a perfect counterpoint to the tartness of the dried fruit.

3 tbs. olive oil
1 clove garlic, minced
½ cup chopped purple onion
2 tbs. curry powder
1 tsp. cumin seeds, toasted and ground (see page 9)
¼ tsp. cayenne pepper
3 cups Arborio rice
6 cups simmering vegetable or fish stock (see page 15, 16)
½ cup grated mozzarella cheese
½ cup golden raisins
¾ cup chopped dried apricots
1 cup frozen peas
1 cup fresh cauliflower florets, broken into tiny pieces, cooked for 5 minutes
3 scallions, chopped, for garnish

In an uncovered pressure cooker, heat olive oil over medium heat. Add garlic and onion and sauté until soft, but not brown. Add curry powder, cumin and cayenne pepper. Stir well. Add Arborio rice and stir to coat all grains with oil. Add stock and stir well. Cover cooker and bring to high pressure; cook for 11 to 12 minutes. Remove from heat, reduce pressure and remove lid. Add mozzarella cheese. Stir to melt cheese and add apricots, peas and cauliflower. Stir to heat. Sprinkle with scallions and serve immediately.

VARIATION
Add fish, shrimp, chicken or beef with the appropriate stock. Serve toasted coconut flakes (see page 9) as an accompaniment.

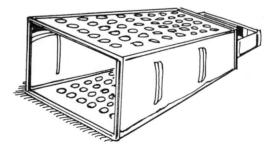

BLACK OLIVE AND SALT COD RISOTTO

Servings: 4-6

Salty, succulent and satisfying, that's what I call this recipe. Salt cod can be purchased in most supermarkets or markets that cater to Mediterranean tastes. It is usually stored in the refrigerated delicatessen department, sometimes in little wooden boxes. Black olives provide an interesting and tasty counterpoint to the fish, and the risotto soaks up the flavors of both with equal intensity. Toasted pine nuts add a delightful crunch.

8 oz. salt cod
cold water
¾ cup milk
2 tbs. butter
2 cloves garlic, minced
2 tsp. olive oil
½ cup minced onion
1 tbs. fennel seeds, toasted (see page 9)

2 cups Arborio rice
4 cups simmering fish stock (see page 16)
1 cup dry white wine
½ cup kalamata or niçoise olives, pitted
1 tbs. grated fresh lemon peel (zest)
1 tbs. butter
3 tbs. pine nuts, toasted (see page 8)

Reconstitute salt cod by placing it in a large bowl of cold water. Change water once or twice, and soak for 6 to 8 hours. Drain water and rinse cod. Cut cod into small pieces and place in a 2-quart saucepan. Cover with cold water and cook over medium heat for about 15 minutes. Drain. With a food processor, process fish, milk, butter and garlic. Set aside.

Heat olive oil in a 2-quart saucepan over medium heat. Add onion and sauté until soft. Add roasted fennel seed and mix well. Add Arborio rice, mixing to coat all grains. Mix fish stock with white wine. Add stock mixture 1 cup at a time. As each cup of stock mixture is absorbed, add more liquid, stirring constantly. Reserve 1/2 cup of the liquid. When grains are soft on the outside, but still have a slightly firm center, *al dente*, add olives, grated lemon peel and mashed cod mixture. Stir in reserved 1/2 cup liquid and 1 tbs. butter. Spoon into warm individual bowls and garnish with toasted pine nuts.

ARTICHOKE RISOTTO

This combination of artichokes, peppers, olives, mushrooms and rice is a winner for all seasons. All of the ingredients can be stored, which makes a spur-of-the-moment invitation easy to extend.

1 red or yellow bell pepper, roasted and peeled (see page 8)
1/4 cup chopped shallots
2 cloves garlic, minced
2 tbs. olive oil
8 oz. fresh mushrooms, sliced
2 pkg. (10 oz. each) frozen artichoke hearts or baby artichokes, thawed and drained
2 tbs. olive oil
1/2 cup minced onion
1 tbs. dried oregano
2 cups Arborio rice
4 cups vegetable or chicken stock (see page 15, 17)
1/4 cup pitted dry-cured black olives
1 tsp. salt
freshly ground pepper to taste
1/2 cup grated Gruyère cheese

Cut roasted pepper in half and lay flat on a cutting board. With a sharp knife, cut into fine strips, about 1/4-inch wide and 2 inches long. Set aside. In a 4-quart pot with a lid, sauté shallots and garlic in 2 tbs. olive oil over medium heat for 2 minutes. Reduce heat to low, cover and cook for 1 minute. Remove cover and add mushrooms and artichoke hearts. Sauté for 5 minutes. Remove cooked mixture from pot and heat 2 tbs. olive oil over medium heat. Add minced onion and sauté until wilted. Add dried oregano and stir to combine. Add Arborio rice and turn to coat all grains with oil. Add vegetable or chicken stock 1 cup at a time, stirring constantly. As liquid is absorbed, add more. Keep stirring rice with a wooden spoon so it does not stick to bottom of pot. When rice grains are still slightly firm at the center, but soft on the outside, *al dente*, return cooked mushroom mixture to pot. Add olives, salt and pepper, and mix thoroughly. Remove from heat and mix in pepper strips and Gruyère. Serve hot.

VARIATION
Add 1/2 lb. cooked shrimp just before serving.

AVOCADO, ROASTED CHILES AND CORN RISOTTO

This is a variation of a Mexican rice dish. In this recipe, we begin with the classic cooking method, but undercook it and finish it off in the oven. You may opt to have it more crunchy in the center of each grain, as is a true risotto. In that case, do not cover the casserole dish when you place the assembled risotto in the oven. It will allow the stock to be absorbed more quickly. Some crusty bread, a cooling salad and a rich chocolate dessert are all you need to round out this hearty dish.

2 poblano chile peppers, roasted and peeled (see page 8)
1 red bell pepper, roasted (see page 8)
2 tbs. corn oil
1/2 cup finely diced onion
2 cloves garlic, minced
2 tsp. cumin seeds, toasted and ground (see page 9)
1 1/2 cups Arborio rice

1 tsp. salt
5 cups hot chicken stock (see page 17)
1 1/2 cups uncooked fresh corn kernels (from 2-3 ears of corn)
1 ripe avocado, peeled, cut into 1/2-inch dice
2 tbs. chopped fresh oregano, or 2 tsp. dried
1 cup grated Reggiano Parmesan cheese

Heat oven to 350°. Slice poblano chiles and red bell pepper into ½-inch strips. Set aside. Heat oil on top of stove in an ovenproof casserole or pot over medium heat. Sauté onion until limp, but not brown. Add garlic and cook for 30 seconds. Add ground cumin and mix well. Add rice and stir to coat all grains with oil. Stir constantly until rice turns light brown. Add salt. Add 3 cups of the hot stock and stir again. Cover casserole and place in oven. Check liquid after 8 to 10 minutes, and add 1 cup stock if liquid has evaporated. Bake for 5 minutes and add remaining stock and corn. Mix well. Return to oven for 3 to 4 minutes, uncovered. Remove from oven and stir in poblano and bell pepper strips, avocado and oregano. Add grated Parmesan cheese and serve immediately.

VARIATION
Serve at room temperature with slices of fresh lime.

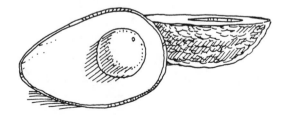

TUNA, GINGER AND CAPER RISOTTO

Servings: 6-8

This dish is a bit more elegant, but just as hearty, as a good old-fashioned tuna casserole. It calls for fish stock, but you can use chicken stock, or a combination of equal amounts of bottled clam juice, water and white wine. Serve it in summer when tomatoes are at their best, with a platter of thickly sliced fresh tomatoes topped with chopped fresh basil and robust olive oil.

2 tbs. olive oil
½ cup finely diced onion
2 cups Arborio rice
1 cup dry white wine
4-5 cups simmering fish stock (see page 16)

1 can (6¾ oz.) tuna fish, flaked
3 tbs. small capers
6 anchovy fillets, chopped
1 tbs. grated ginger root
⅓ cup chopped fresh cilantro, optional
salt and freshly ground pepper to taste

Heat olive oil in an uncovered pressure cooker over medium heat. Add onion and sauté until wilted. Add rice and stir until all grains are coated with oil. Add white wine and 3 cups of the hot fish stock. Cover pressure cooker and bring to a high pressure. Cook for 6 minutes. Remove from heat, release pressure and remove lid. Add remaining stock, tuna, capers, anchovies and ginger. Secure lid and bring pressure to medium. Cook for 2 to 3 minutes. Remove from heat, reduce pressure and remove lid. Add cilantro, if using, salt and pepper. Serve hot or at room temperature.

GREMOLATA RISOTTO

Servings:

Here is a risotto to serve alone or to accompany braised veal shanks. Gremolata is a fragrant mixture of minced garlic, parsley and lemon peel that is usually sprinkled over the meat just before serving. It is added to the risotto in this recipe.

2 cloves garlic
1/2 cup chopped fresh flat-leaf parsley
grated peel of 1 lemon or orange (zest)
4 anchovy fillets, optional
2 tbs. butter
1 tbs. olive oil or anchovy oil

1/2 cup finely diced onion
3 cups Arborio rice
7 cups simmering beef or chicken stock
  (see page 18, 17)
1 cup grated Reggiano Parmesan cheese

Chop garlic, parsley, lemon peel and anchovies with a sharp knife or a food processor. Do not mash into a paste —the tiny pieces should be dry enough to sprinkle into the finished risotto. In a 4-quart heavy saucepan, melt butter with oil over medium heat. Add chopped onion and sauté until wilted. Do not brown. Add Arborio rice. Stir rice, coating all grains with fat. Add hot stock, about 1 cup at a time. Keep stirring rice as it cooks. As each cup of stock is absorbed, add next cup. Continue process until grains are cooked *al dente,* or slightly firm in the center and soft on the outside. Fold in grated Parmesan cheese. Stir in gremolata and serve at once on heated plates or bowls.

SWISS CHARD RISOTTO

One of my favorite leafy vegetables is Swiss chard. I like its slightly bitter quality, and the way it marries beautifully with rice. For large leaves, the stem and center rib should be removed all the way through the leaf. Chop into 1-inch pieces, and precook these pieces. If you are using young Swiss chard, which is more tender, it is not necessary to remove stems and center ribs.

1 lb. fresh tomatoes
2 tbs. tomato paste
3 lb. Swiss chard
3 large cloves garlic, minced
2 medium yellow onions, finely diced
1/4 cup olive oil
1 tbs. dried oregano
1 tsp. dried mint
1 cup Arborio rice

3 cups simmering chicken or vegetable
  stock (see page 17, 15)
2 tbs. chopped fresh oregano
1/2 tsp. salt
1/4 tsp. freshly ground pepper
1/2 cup grated Reggiano Parmesan
  cheese

Cut tomatoes in half and squeeze out seeds. Place in a food processor workbowl and process briefly to a coarse puree. Add tomato paste and process until smooth. Remove stems from Swiss chard and chop stems and leaves separately into bite-sized pieces. Cook stems in boiling water for 2 minutes. Drain. Mix stems and leaves with contents of food processor and set aside. Sauté garlic and onion in olive oil in a large sauté pan over medium heat. Add dried oregano and mint. Reduce heat to low, cover and cook until onion is soft and transparent. Add rice and turn to coat all grains with oil. Add hot stock, about 1 cup at a time, stirring constantly. As stock is absorbed, add more stock. Repeat until grains are soft on the outside and somewhat firm in the middle, *all dente*. Add Swiss chard mixture, combining well with rice. Cover and cook for 1 minute. Add fresh oregano. Add salt and pepper. Taste and adjust seasonings if necessary. Add Parmesan cheese just before serving.

VARIATION

To make this recipe into an entrée, add 2 cups cooked ground or chopped lamb or chicken about 10 minutes before rice is done.

RISOTTO WITH ANCHOVIES AND CREAM

Servings: 4-6

Salty anchovies, silky cream and soothing risotto — this is a recipe for true anchovy lovers. The anchovies will essentially dissolve into the cream and rice, leaving only their intense flavor. The rice will absorb liquid as it sits, so if you are planning to serve it as soon as it is done, you will need less cream.

1 can (4 oz.) anchovy fillets, drained, oil reserved
1 tbs. olive oil, or more
1 large sweet onion, minced
3 cloves garlic, minced
1/2 cup sliced leeks, white part only
11/2 cups Arborio rice
4 cups hot fish or chicken stock (see page 16, 17)
1/2-1 cup warm heavy cream
1 cup fresh breadcrumbs, optional
2 tbs. butter or margarine, melted, optional
2 tbs. chopped fresh flat-leaf parsley for garnish, optional

Chop anchovies with a knife or cut into small pieces with scissors. Combine anchovy oil with olive oil to equal 3 tbs., adding more olive oil if necessary. Heat combined oils in a 3-quart saucepan and add onion, garlic and leeks. Cook over medium heat until soft. Add chopped anchovies, pressing them into vegetables.

When anchovies have dissolved slightly, add Arborio rice and mix well to coat all grains with oil. Add 1 cup of the hot stock to rice, stirring mixture well. Continue to stir while rice cooks. As liquid is absorbed, add more stock. Add warm cream when rice is almost fully cooked. Stir well. When the center of each grain is still slightly firm and the outside is soft, *al dente*, rice is done. If desired, spoon rice into a large casserole and sprinkle with fresh breadcrumbs. Drizzle with melted butter and place casserole under a broiler until crumbs are brown. Or, spoon risotto into warm individual bowls and garnish with parsley.

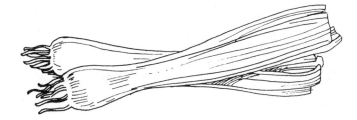

OTTO WITH TOASTED WALNUTS,
IL AND ZUCCHINI

alnuts are especially good in this risotto. Their tastiness is enhanced by toasting, and zucchini provides a balance of texture and flavor. This is a fine accompaniment to sautéed veal or roast chicken, or it can be eaten as a main course when preceded by soup or salad.

2 tbs. olive oil
2 cups diced zucchini, 1/2-inch dice
1/2 cup minced purple onion
1 clove garlic, minced or pressed
1 1/2 cups Arborio rice
6-7 cups simmering vegetable or chicken stock (see page 15, 17)
1 cup coarsely chopped fresh basil leaves
2 tbs. butter, melted
salt and pepper to taste
1 cup grated Reggiano Parmesan cheese
1 cup walnuts, toasted and coarsely chopped (see page 9)

Heat olive oil in a 4-quart pot and sauté zucchini over medium-high heat until cooked through, about 5 minutes. Remove zucchini from pot and add onion and garlic. Sauté over medium heat until soft. Add Arborio rice and mix well to coat all grains with olive oil. Add hot stock, about 1 cup at a time, stirring constantly. As each cup is absorbed, add the next. When rice is slightly firm at the center and soft on the outside, *al dente*, return zucchini to pot. Mix well and add basil and melted butter. Add salt, pepper, grated Parmesan cheese and toasted walnuts. Spoon into warm individual bowls.

SMOKED SALMON RISOTTO WITH FENNEL

Servings: 6

Serve this appetizer with thinly sliced, buttered pumpernickel or rye bread and a chilled bottle of white wine. It can be made well ahead of time, but I recommend letting the rice mixture come to room temperature before you assemble the plates to encourage the flavors to develop.

2 tbs. butter
1 cup diced fresh fennel bulb, leaves reserved
½ cup minced onion
1 cup Arborio rice
2 cups fish or chicken stock (see page 16, 17)
4 oz. chunk smoked salmon, broken into small pieces
2 tbs. flavored rice vinegar or white wine vinegar
1 tbs. grated fresh lemon peel (zest)
3 tbs. drained capers
arugula or spinach leaves, washed and dried
lemon slices for garnish

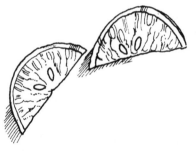

Melt butter in an uncovered pressure cooker over medium heat. Add diced fennel and onion and sauté for 5 minutes or until soft. Add Arborio rice and stir to coat all grains with butter. Add fish stock. Cover pot, bring pressure to high and cook for 11 minutes. Remove from heat, reduce pressure and remove lid. Place contents in a bowl and add smoked salmon, vinegar, lemon peel and capers. Allow rice mixture to cool to room temperature. Roll arugula or spinach leaves into tight cylinders and cut into ¼-inch slices. On each individual serving plate, place some of the sliced greens in a mound. Distribute risotto on greens and garnish with a few feathery leaves of fennel and lemon slices.

Note: To make a lemon twist, slice a lemon into thin rounds. Cut a notch from the edge to the center of each slice. This will make the slice flexible enough to twist.

PINK GRAPEFRUIT AND SCALLOP RISOTTO

Servings: 6

Scallops and grapefruit seem to have a natural affinity for each other. The tartness of the grapefruit is mellowed by the fresh seafood taste, and the spinach provides a slight bitter flavor. The risotto is laced with grated grapefruit peel and parsley and is cooked with some of the citrus juice. The result is a well-balanced, visually beautiful appetizer.

3 pink grapefruits
2 tbs. butter
2 medium cucumbers, peeled, seeded
    and cut into thin matchstick strips
salt and freshly ground pepper to taste
3 tsp. chopped fresh flat-leaf parsley
1-2 tbs. butter or vegetable oil, optional
18-24 sea scallops
2 tsp. flour
1½ cups dry white wine
2 cups cooked spinach, seasoned with
    salt, pepper and nutmeg

2 tbs. butter
1 tbs. olive oil
½ cup minced shallots
½ cup chopped leeks, white part only
1½ cups Arborio rice
5 cups simmering fish or chicken stock
    (see page 16, 17)
1 tbs. grated fresh grapefruit peel (zest)
salt and freshly ground pepper to taste

With a thin sharp knife, cut peel and pith from 2 of the grapefruits to expose pink fruit underneath. Over a bowl, run knife down both sides of the membrane that separates the grapefruit segments and release segments and juice into bowl. Drain segments and reserve juice. If you do not have 1 cup grapefruit juice, squeeze juice from remaining fruit to equal 1 cup. Melt 2 tbs. butter in a large sauté pan over medium heat and sauté cucumber strips until limp, about 5 minutes. Taste for seasonings and add salt and pepper. Remove from heat and add parsley. Transfer to a bowl and set aside. Add more butter or vegetable oil to sauté pan if needed. Roll scallops in flour and sauté over high heat. Remove when firm, about 2 minutes. Add wine to pan, scraping up any bits on bottom of pan. Cook over high heat until wine is reduced by half. Strain and reserve.

Melt 2 tbs. butter with 1 tbs. olive oil in a 3-quart pot over medium heat. Add shallots and leeks and sauté until soft. Add rice and stir to coat all grains with fat. Add hot stock, about 1 cup at a time, stirring constantly. As each cup is absorbed, add another cup. When rice has been cooking for 10 minutes, add 1 cup grapefruit juice. Continue to add hot stock until rice is *al dente*, with the center of each grain still slightly firm and the outside soft. Stir in grapefruit peel, salt and pepper and assemble on individual plates: warm spinach on the bottom, a mound of risotto, topped with 3 or four segments of grapefruit alternating with scallops. Pour a little of the reduced wine over each plate and serve.

GOLDEN RISOTTO

This is a dish to brighten any day. Golden yellow peppers are blended with the initial onion and garlic flavoring, and the flavor is further boosted by the addition of saffron. Serve it as a first course, or if you prefer, as a side dish with a light veal entrée and sautéed fresh spinach.

1/4 tsp. saffron threads
1/4 cup dry white wine
3 yellow bell peppers
2 tbs. butter
1 tbs. olive oil
1/2 cup minced onion
2-3 cloves garlic, minced
2 cups Arborio rice
5 cups simmering chicken stock (see page 17)
1 cup grated Reggiano Parmesan cheese

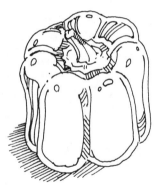

Crush saffron threads with the back of a spoon and soak in wine. Set aside. Mince ½ of the yellow peppers, and cut remaining peppers into thin matchstick strips. Heat butter and olive oil in a 3-quart pot over medium heat. Add onion and garlic and sauté briefly until soft. Add minced bell pepper and cook for 1 to 2 minutes. Add Arborio rice and stir to coat all grains with fat. Combine saffron and wine with chicken stock. Add 1 cup of the hot stock mixture to rice. Continue to stir mixture, and as each cup of liquid is absorbed, add more. Add bell pepper strips to pot and mix thoroughly. When grains of rice are still slightly firm in the center, but soft on the outside, *al dente*, add ½ cup of the Parmesan cheese. Serve in warm individual shallow bowls, or in a large serving bowl, and pass remaining Parmesan cheese.

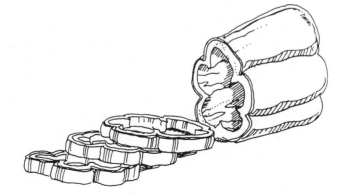

HAM, CANTALOUPE AND PINE NUT RISOTTO   Servings: 6

Prosciutto is the ham of choice for this recipe, preferably Italian. You can substitute any dry cured local ham. Use cantaloupe or honeydew melon.

2 tbs. butter
1 tbs. olive oil
½ onion, minced
¾ cup finely diced carrots
¾ cup diced fresh fennel bulb
6 oz. chunk prosciutto, finely diced
1 cup Arborio rice
4 cups simmering chicken or vegetable
    stock (see page 17, 15)

3 tbs. Marsala wine
½ cup sliced oil-cured black olives
1 cup diced melon
½ cup grated Reggiano Parmesan cheese
salt and freshly ground pepper to taste
1-2 melons, cut into 18 thin slices
12 very thin slices prosciutto
¼ cup toasted pine nuts for garnish
    (see page 8)

Heat butter and olive oil in a 3-quart saucepan over medium heat. Add onion, carrots, fennel and prosciutto and sauté until vegetables are soft. Add rice, turning to coat all grains with fat. Add hot stock 1 cup at a time, continually stirring rice. As each cup is absorbed, add more stock. When grains are still slightly firm in the center, but soft on the outside, *al dente*, add Marsala. Cook for 1 minute. Remove risotto from heat and mix in olives, diced melon and Parmesan. Add salt and pepper, if needed. Fan out 3 melon slices on each plate. Place a mound of risotto in inner curve of melon slices. Drape prosciutto slices over risotto and sprinkle each serving with pine nuts.

FENNEL RISOTTO

The pressure cooker saves time and pot-watching. The taste of the fennel is enhanced by the tarragon and the creaminess of the rice is savory and satisfying. Serve it with your favorite roast pork loin recipe and lemon-flavored applesauce.

2 tbs. butter
1 tbs. vegetable oil
1 tbs. dried tarragon
1/2 cup diced onion
3/4 cup chopped fresh fennel bulb

1 1/2 cups Arborio rice
3 cups chicken stock (see page 17)
1 tsp. salt
1/2 cup grated Reggiano Parmesan cheese

Melt butter with oil in an uncovered pressure cooker over medium heat. Add tarragon, onion and fennel. Cook for 3 to 4 minutes, until onion is soft. Add Arborio rice, stirring to coat all grains with fat. Add chicken stock and salt. Cover pressure cooker, bring to high pressure and cook for 12 minutes. Remove from heat, reduce pressure and remove lid. Grains of rice should be slightly firm at the center and soft on the outside, *al dente*. Add 1/2 cup grated Parmesan cheese and serve at once, with more Parmesan on the side.

VARIATION

Add 8 oz. mushrooms, quartered, sautéed in butter, to risotto just before serving.

EMERALD RISOTTO

This recipe lives up to its name. It has a lovely green color, and the jalapeño pepper adds just enough zing to get one's attention. Serve it with grilled chicken and a garnish of thinly sliced melon and you have a perfect summer meal.

3 tbs. olive oil
1 large onion, chopped
2 cloves garlic, chopped
1 jalapeño chile pepper, seeded and minced
2 cups Arborio rice
4 cups simmering chicken stock (see page 17)
salt and freshly ground pepper to taste
½ cup chopped fresh cilantro
½ cup chopped fresh flat-leaf parsley
½ cup chopped fresh spinach

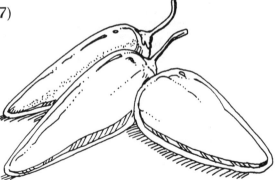

In an uncovered pressure cooker over medium heat, heat oil; add chopped onion and garlic. Sauté for 3 to 4 minutes and add jalapeño pepper. Sauté for 1 to 2 minutes and add rice. Mix to coat all grains with fat. Add hot stock, salt and freshly ground pepper. Cover, bring to high pressure and cook for 6 minutes. Remove from heat, reduce pressure, remove lid and add chopped cilantro, parsley and spinach. Cook without pressure, stirring frequently, until grains are slightly firm at the center and soft on the outside, *al dente*. Taste for seasonings and adjust, if necessary.

VARIATIONS

- Add 2 tbs. lemon juice and a sprinkling of olive oil; serve cold.
- Add slivered cooked ham or chicken, or shrimp.
- Add cooked green peas.
- Add thin strips of sautéed fresh fennel bulb and cooked spiced ground beef, topped with a spoonful of sour cream or yogurt and chopped scallions for each serving.

SOUTHWESTERN SALSA RISOTTO

Servings: 6-8

Tomatillos, fresh tomatoes, cilantro and cooked risotto infused with piquant herbs and spices jolt the appetite to sit up and take notice. The risotto serves as a conductor of these flavors. It is a refreshing first course, and can be served hot or cold. If you prefer, chop tomatillos, tomatoes and onion with a food processor. Remove brown hulls from tomatillos and rinse well in warm water before dicing.

2 cups diced tomatillos
1½ cups chopped peeled, seeded plum
  (Roma) tomatoes (see page 7)
½ cup diced onion
2 cloves garlic, minced
½ jalapeño chile pepper, seeds and
  ribs removed, minced
3 tbs. lime juice
½ cup chopped fresh cilantro leaves
½ tsp. salt
2 tbs. olive oil
1 tbs. butter

½ cup minced onion
1 clove garlic, pressed
1 tsp. turmeric
1 tsp. cumin seeds, toasted and ground
  (see page 9)
1 cup Arborio rice
3 cups simmering vegetable or chicken
  stock (see page 15, 17)
hot pepper sauce to taste, optional
additional cumin and minced garlic,
  optional
lime slices for garnish

Combine tomatillos with tomatoes, ½ cup diced onion, 2 cloves garlic, jalapeño, lime juice, cilantro and salt; set aside. Heat olive oil and butter in an uncovered pressure cooker over medium heat. Add ½ cup diced onion and 1 clove garlic and cook until soft. Stir in turmeric and cumin, mixing well. Add Arborio rice and turn to coat all grains with fat. Add vegetable stock. Place lid on pot and bring up to high pressure. Cook for 12 minutes. Remove from heat, reduce pressure and remove cover. Add tomatillo mixture to cooked risotto and mix well. Taste for seasoning, and add hot pepper sauce and more cumin and garlic if desired. Serve on individual plates, garnished with lime slices.

FRUIT RISOTTO

Here is a combination of rum-soaked dried apricots, golden raisins and plump prunes added to a risotto that is cooked with ginger-flavored milk. It is best eaten warm or at room temperature. In this recipe, we use a rice cooker. It steams the rice, and can hold the pudding for several hours with little or no loss of flavor. Although risotto usually has firm-centered grains, what we are looking for in this recipe is the creaminess of the short-grain Arborio rice. The texture will be soft, enhanced by the aroma and chewiness of the dried fruits.

½ cup diced dried apricots
½ cup golden raisins
½ cup halved small pitted prunes
½ cup dark rum
2 cups hot milk
1 tbs. grated ginger root

2 tbs. butter
1 cup Arborio rice
2 tbs. sugar
½ tsp. ground cardamom
¼ cup chopped candied ginger
Rum Custard Sauce, follows

Soak dried apricots, raisins and prunes in rum for at least 30 minutes. Spray a rice cooker with nonstick cooking spray and turn it on. Add hot milk, grated ginger, butter, rice, sugar and ground cardamom to cooker. Cover and cook until machine turns off. Remove cover, avoiding hot steam, and add rum-soaked dried fruits and candied ginger. Mix well. Spoon into individual serving bowls and pass *Rum Custard Sauce*.

RUM CUSTARD SAUCE

This is a light, pourable custard, sometimes called "crème anglaise." It can be flavored with vanilla instead of liquor, and dresses up a rice pudding in a very elegant way.

4 egg yolks
⅓ cup sugar
1½ cups milk

2 tbs. flour
2 tbs. rum

In a bowl, combine egg yolks with sugar. Beat until frothy. In a 1-quart saucepan, mix ½ cup of the milk with 2 tbs. flour and stir until flour is dissolved. Add remaining milk and heat until slightly thickened, stirring continuously. Pour a little of the hot milk into beaten egg mixture, and stir to combine well. Pour egg mixture into heating milk, and continue to cook until sauce thickens. Keep heat low and stir continuously. When consistency is similar to a thick milk shake and coats the spoon, remove from heat and strain immediately, while still hot. Add rum and serve immediately.

RICE APPETIZERS

COCONUT BEEF PILLOWS

These pillow-shaped hors d'oeuvres are winners. They freeze very well, unbaked. Do not defrost before baking.

1 cup chopped fresh spinach, or frozen, thawed
1 small onion, chopped
2 cloves garlic, minced
6 tbs. olive oil
2 tbs. curry powder

½ cup unsweetened flaked coconut
3 cups shredded or chopped cooked beef or other meat
1 cup cooked risotto (see pages 13-23)
salt and freshly ground pepper to taste
1 pkg. (16 oz.) phyllo dough, thawed

Heat oven to 350°. For fresh spinach, steam briefly, chop and drain well. For frozen spinach, drain and squeeze dry. Sauté onion and garlic in 2 tbs. of the olive oil over medium heat until onion is soft. Add curry powder and sauté briefly. Remove from heat and combine with spinach, coconut, beef, risotto, salt and pepper. Taste for seasonings, and adjust if necessary. Cut phyllo dough in half lengthwise, and cut each half crosswise into thirds. Keep unused phyllo covered with plastic wrap and a damp towel. Place 4 rectangles of dough side by side, brush with remaining olive oil, and cover each with another piece of phyllo. Brush again with oil. Place 2 tbs. filling in the center of the short edge of each rectangle, fold the sides in toward the center and roll up. Place on a greased baking sheet and brush with oil. Bake for 20 to 25 minutes.

FIG, PROSCIUTTO AND CAPER TARTS

Yield: about 42

Fresh figs and prosciutto are a perfect gastronomic duo. The chewiness of the ham and the soft texture of the figs are further enhanced when combined with this aromatic caper and Parmesan cheese risotto.

1 pkg. (17.25 oz.) frozen puff pastry dough, thawed
2 cups cooked risotto (see pages 13-23)
½ cup grated Reggiano Parmesan cheese
1 cup low-fat sour cream
1 cup low-fat plain yogurt
2 tbs. Dijon mustard
2 tbs. pureed capers
2 cloves garlic, minced
salt and freshly ground pepper to taste
20 medium-sized fresh black figs
1 cup thinly sliced prosciutto
shaved Reggiano Parmesan cheese, optional

Heat oven to 350°. Fit dough into a 9-x-12-inch rectangular tart pan with a removable bottom. With a fork, prick dough all over, and cover with a piece of aluminum foil. Weight foil down with metal pie weights or dried beans and bake for 15 to 20 minutes. Remove aluminum foil and weights and deflate dough, if it has puffed up, by pricking again with a fork. Bake tart shell until light brown and dry. It should take another 10 minutes. Cool tart shell.

Combine cooked risotto, grated cheese, sour cream, yogurt, mustard, capers and garlic. Taste for seasoning and add salt and pepper if desired. Spread mixture on cooled tart shell. Slice figs in half or quarters and arrange in an attractive pattern on top of risotto mixture. Sprinkle prosciutto slices over tart, and add shavings of Parmesan cheese, if using. Cut into bite-sized squares just before serving.

VARIATION

For a luncheon dish, cut the tart into larger portions and garnish with fresh orange slices.

LAMB CURRY "SNAILS"

These are scrumptious hors d'oeuvres. Keep them unbaked in your freezer until needed, and you have the beginning of a great party. You can use fresh, uncooked ground lamb, or the trimmings from a cooked lamb roast. Use prepared puff pastry, available in the frozen food section of your local supermarket. In a pinch, you can also use pie dough or phyllo dough, but puff pastry really absorbs the flavors of the filling better.

1 pkg. (17.25 oz.) puff pastry dough, thawed
½ cup fennel seeds
1 tbs. olive oil
2 cloves garlic, minced
1 medium onion, chopped
2 tbs. curry powder
1 tbs. cumin seeds, toasted and ground (see page 8)
2 cups uncooked lean ground lamb, or 2 cups chopped cooked lamb
1 cup cooked short-grain rice (see page 10)
salt and freshly ground pepper to taste
additional garlic, optional
½ cup cooked or frozen green peas, optional
1 egg yolk mixed with 1 tbs. milk or cream

Prepare filling: Heat olive oil in a large sauté pan over medium heat. Add onion and garlic and sauté until soft. Add curry powder and ground cumin, and mix well into onion. Add lamb and sauté until no longer pink. When lamb is fully cooked, drain juices from pan, add cooked rice and taste for seasoning. Add more curry powder, cumin and garlic if necessary. Add salt and pepper. Add peas, if using. Cool mixture.

Line a baking sheet with parchment or waxed paper. Roll out 1 puff pastry sheet on a wooden board that has been dusted with flour and sprinkled with $\frac{1}{2}$ of the fennel seeds. Cut sheet in half the long way, that is, parallel with the lower edge of the board. Place a line of filling midway up from the bottom of the dough. Fold the top third of the dough down over the filling, leaving 1 inch of dough uncovered along the bottom edge. Press edges together to seal in filling. Cut 1-inch pieces from the roll, and place them on edge on baking sheet. The filling will show on both sides. Each hors d'oeuvre will look like a cross section of a snail in its shell, the 1-inch uncovered piece of dough being the body of the snail. Freeze or chill for at least 1 hour before baking.

Heat oven to 375°. Brush pastry with egg yolk mixture and bake for about 20 minutes, or until cooked through and pastry is slightly brown. If you plan to use these at a later time, freeze them unbaked and take them directly from freezer to the oven.

MOROCCAN CIGARETTES

Yield: about 8 dozen

These spicy, slender hors d'oeuvres are always a hit. They should be highly seasoned, so be sure to taste and adjust the flavor before you fill them. The risotto binds the ingredients together, and makes them easier to eat, as they are quite fragile to hold. Roll them as compactly as you can, or they will turn into cigars! After they are assembled, you can freeze the "cigarettes" until ready to bake.

3 tbs. olive oil
1 leek, white part only, chopped
½ cup minced onion
4 cloves garlic, minced
⅛ tsp. cayenne pepper
2 tbs. cumin seeds, toasted and ground (see page 8)
1 tsp. curry powder
¼ tsp. ground allspice
6 cups grated carrots
1 cup dried currants
1½ cups cooked risotto (see pages 13-23)
salt and freshly ground pepper to taste
1 pkg. (1 lb.) phyllo dough, thawed
½ cup butter, melted, mixed with ½ cup vegetable oil

Heat olive oil in a very large sauté pan over medium heat and add leek, onion and garlic. Sauté for 3 to 4 minutes, and add cayenne pepper, cumin, curry powder and allspice. Cook for 2 minutes to blend flavors. Add carrots.

Cook, stirring frequently, until carrots are cooked and wilted. Add currants and continue to cook for 5 minutes. Add risotto and mix to distribute ingredients evenly. Add salt and pepper. Taste and adjust seasonings. Cool mixture. This filling can be made 1 to 2 days ahead, or even frozen.

Heat oven to 350° and line a baking sheet with oiled parchment paper. Cut phyllo dough into 4½-inch squares. (Phyllo dough trimmings can be pieced together and filled in the same way.) Keep unused dough covered with plastic wrap and a damp cloth. Brush a square of dough with butter-oil mixture and place a line of filling (about 2 tbs., or less) across lower edge of dough. Roll it up as tightly as you can and place roll on baking sheet. Brush roll with butter-oil mixture. Repeat until all filling is used. Bake for 15 minutes, or until brown.

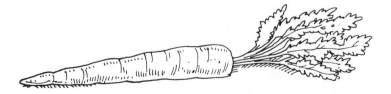

PORTOBELLO MUSHROOM CALZETTES

Yield: about 36

This cutesy name (sorry!) describes a 3-inch hors d'oeuvre. Braised napa cabbage (sometimes called Chinese cabbage) is a perfect counterpoint to the meaty flavor of the Portobello mushrooms. Mascarpone cheese is a very rich, creamy Italian cheese that makes this pastry dough tender.

1 cup rye flour
2 cups all-purpose flour
1 tsp. salt
2 tbs. caraway seeds, toasted and ground (see page 9)
2 tbs. cold butter, cut into small pieces
½ cup mascarpone cheese
⅔ cup plain yogurt (can be low-fat)
3 tbs. olive oil
½ cup diced onion
2-3 cloves garlic, minced
1 medium napa cabbage, thinly sliced
salt and freshly ground pepper to taste
1 cup thinly sliced Portobello mushrooms
½ cup very thinly sliced Genoa salami or prosciutto
2 cups cooked long-grain rice (see page 10)

Place rye flour, all-purpose flour, salt, 1 tbs. of the ground caraway seeds, and butter in a food processor workbowl. Pulse until butter is completely combined with dry ingredients. Add mascarpone cheese and yogurt and process until a ball of dough forms. Remove dough and dust with flour. Place dough in a plastic bag and let it rest for at least 30 minutes in a cool place. (Or place dry ingredients in a bowl, cut in butter with a pastry cutter or fork, add cheese and yogurt and stir until dough forms a mass.)

Heat 2 tbs. olive oil in a large sauté pan over medium heat and add onion, garlic and remaining ground caraway seeds. Cook until soft. Add napa cabbage, sautéing until wilted. You may have to lower heat and place a lid on the pan. The cabbage will exude a lot of juice. Cook cabbage until very limp. Drain cabbage mixture, transfer to a bowl and return liquids to pan. Reduce liquid by half and pour it over cabbage mixture. Add salt and pepper to taste, and set mixture aside. Add remaining 1 tbs. olive oil to pan and sauté mushrooms over high heat until cooked through, about 5 minutes. Add mushrooms, salami and rice to cabbage mixture. Cool before using.

Heat oven to 350°. Line a baking sheet with oiled parchment or waxed paper. Roll dough out as thinly as possible on a floured board. Cut out 3-inch rounds and brush dough with water. Place 1 heaping tbs. filling in the center of each round, and fold dough over to form a half-moon. Crimp edges. Repeat with remaining filling. Place calzettes on baking sheet, prick all over with a fork, and bake for 20 to 25 minutes, turning once to brown both sides. Serve warm or at room temperature.

MUSHROOM CAPS WITH
SMOKED OYSTERS AND RICE

Yield: 24

If stuffed mushrooms seem old hat to you, try these. The smokiness of the oysters seems just perfect for the subtle taste of the mushroom caps. Rice, once again, is the magic that makes it work — satisfying without being filling, and appetizing without being overpowering. This may become one of your favorite hors d'oeuvres.

24 large mushroom caps
1 tbs. butter
2 tsp. dried thyme
½ tsp. salt
1 cup cooked brown rice (see page 10)

3 tbs. minced fresh flat-leaf parsley
1 can (4 oz.) smoked oysters, minced
1 clove garlic, minced
½ cup grated Gruyère cheese
salt and freshly ground pepper to taste

Heat oven to 350°. Wipe large mushroom caps with a damp towel to clean thoroughly. Heat butter in a large skillet and sauté mushroom caps over high heat until golden. Turn once. Sprinkle with 1 tsp. of the thyme and salt and remove from pan. Drain upside down on paper towels. Mix brown rice with chopped parsley, minced oysters, garlic, remaining thyme and Gruyère cheese, reserving some of the cheese to sprinkle on tops of stuffing. Add salt and pepper. Fill mushroom caps, sprinkle with remaining cheese and bake for 20 minutes.

STUFFED CURRIED MUSSELS

Here is a colorful and attractive hors d'oeuvre that can be passed or set on a buffet table. The bright curried rice forms an appetizing platform for the cooked mussels, which are then garnished with chives. Find out how to clean and cook mussels on page 97, where they are featured in a salad.

30 cooked mussels
2 tbs. minced garlic
1 cup mayonnaise
1 tsp. curry powder
1/2 tsp. cumin seeds, toasted and
    ground (see page 9)

3 cups *Curried Risotto* (see page 42)
salt and freshly ground pepper to taste
fresh chives or scallion tops, cut into
    1-inch pieces

Remove cooked mussels from shells. Reserve shells and meat separately. Fold garlic into mayonnaise and add curry and cumin. Reserve 1/2 cup of the garlic mayonnaise to coat mussels; combine remaining 1/2 cup mayonnaise mixture with risotto. Pack 1 tbs. of the rice into a mussel shell and top with a mussel that has been coated in garlic mayonnaise. Garnish with a piece of chive set at an angle. Or, separate mussel shells into 2 pieces, fill one half and place unused half of mussel shell into filled half, sticking up at an angle. This can be used as a "shovel" to scoop out the contents of the filled shell.

CRAB BUNDLES

This recipe is best when it is made with fresh lump crabmeat, free of cartilage, and not previously frozen. You will find it chilled in the refrigerator case of your supermarket or fish store. Very fresh crab in season is full of flavor, and when combined with the other ingredients in this recipe makes an outstanding dish.

1 tbs. olive oil
1 leek, white part only, cleaned and
    thinly sliced into rings
3 cloves garlic, crushed
2 tsp. curry powder
1/2 tsp. sweet paprika
12 oz. fresh crabmeat
3/4 cup cooked short-grain rice (see
    page 10)
1/3 cup frozen peas, not thawed

1/2 tsp. dry mustard
1 tsp. minced ginger root
1 large egg, beaten
salt and freshly ground pepper to taste
16 sheets phyllo dough, each 8 1/2
    inches square
1/4 cup butter, melted
8 chives or scallion tops about 10
    inches long
Roasted Red Pepper Sauce, follows

Heat oven to 350°. Heat olive oil in a medium sauté pan over medium heat and sauté leek and garlic until wilted. Add curry powder and paprika and mix briefly. Remove from heat and add crabmeat, rice, peas, dry mustard, ginger, egg, salt and pepper; mix well.

Line a baking sheet with oiled parchment or waxed paper. Place 1 square of phyllo dough on a work surface. (Cover unused phyllo with plastic wrap and a damp cloth.) Brush with melted butter. Cover with another phyllo square, with corners diagonal, making an eight-pointed star. Place a heaping ⅓ cup of filling in the center of star. Pull up corners to meet over filling; twist slightly. The bundle will resemble a pouch. Tie a chive around neck of pouch, making a bow. Brush pouch with melted butter and place on baking sheet. Bake for about 35 minutes, or until lightly browned. Repeat for remaining phyllo and filling. Serve with *Roasted Red Pepper Sauce*.

ROASTED RED PEPPER SAUCE

When served cold, this sauce can be mixed with mayonnaise, yogurt or sour cream. You can thin it with stock and/or heavy cream, and serve it either hot or cold. This will keep for about 1 week in the refrigerator.

2 large red bell peppers, roasted (see page 8)
1 clove garlic
1 tsp. capers

1 tbs. curry powder
½ cup chicken stock or dry white wine
½ cup heavy cream
salt and pepper

Place all ingredients in a food processor workbowl. Process briefly and taste for seasoning. Heat gently for use as a warm sauce, as the cream separates easily.

STUFFED GRAPE LEAVES WITH A TWIST

Yield: 24

Ground hazelnuts are an unusual addition to these succulent little packages. They can be presented as appetizers, or as part of a vegetarian or even a cross-ethnic buffet. It is important to use a good quality fruity olive oil, and that the cumin be freshly toasted and ground. The grape leaves can be purchased in Middle Eastern food stores or in the ethnic foods section of your supermarket.

2 cups cooked risotto (see pages 13-23)
2 tbs. cumin seeds, toasted and ground
(see page 9)
1 cup ground toasted hazelnuts (see
page 8)
3 tbs. pressed garlic
1 tsp. salt

$\frac{1}{4}$ tsp. cayenne pepper
2 tbs. lemon juice
$\frac{1}{2}$ cup olive oil
1 jar (16 oz.) grape leaves in brine,
rinsed and patted dry
1 cup plain yogurt, thinned with 1 tbs.
lemon juice

Heat oven to 350°. Oil a rimmed baking sheet. Combine all ingredients, except grape leaves and yogurt, reserving $\frac{1}{4}$ cup of the olive oil. Snip off and discard any tough stem ends of grape leaves. Place leaves flat on a counter, inside up. Place about 2 tbs. filling along the base of each leaf, turn sides of leaf in, and roll up tightly. Place packets close together on baking sheet. Brush with remaining oil and bake for 30 minutes. Serve at room temperature or refrigerate for later use. Serve with yogurt-lemon mixture.

RICE SALADS AND SOUPS

SCANDINAVIAN SALAD WITH RISOTTO

Servings: 6

A classic salad of beets, potatoes and pickled herring tops warm risotto. The rice absorbs and extends the various flavors in a very pleasing and tasty way. Tiny cucumber pickles, called gherkins, are cut into fan shapes for attractive garnishes.

8 oz. drained herring fillets, cut into ½-inch dice
1 cup diced peeled, boiled potatoes, ½-inch dice
½ cup diced cooked beets
1 cup minced sweet onion
1 cup diced peeled Granny Smith apples, ½-inch dice
2 hard-cooked eggs
2 tbs. chopped fresh dill
1 cup *Aioli,* follows
salt and freshly ground pepper to taste
shredded Romaine lettuce
3 cups warm cooked risotto (see pages 13-23)
6 small gherkins for garnish

Combine herring, potatoes, beets, onion and apples. Cut eggs in half, remove yolks, push them through a sieve and set aside. Dice egg whites and add to herring-potato mixture. Add dill and *Aioli*. Taste for seasoning and add salt and freshly ground pepper. Place a base of lettuce on each of 6 salad plates. Mound 1/2 cup warm risotto on each lettuce base. Spoon herring-potato mixture over rice and sprinkle with sieved egg yolks. Make fan shapes from gherkins: hold each gherkin at one end, and cut 3 or 4 slices the long way, leaving the end you are holding uncut. Spread slices into a fan shape. Garnish salads with fanned gherkins.

AIOLI
1 cup purchased mayonnaise
1/4 cup fish stock or white wine
2-3 cloves garlic, minced

Mix all ingredients together until well blended.

ASIAN SESAME RICE SALAD

This is a variation of an Asian noodle dish. The flavors are boosted by the addition of tahini, or sesame paste. Tahini is available in Middle Eastern markets, in specialty gourmet stores and some supermarkets.

3 tbs. sesame oil
½ onion, minced
2 cloves garlic, minced
3 tbs. tahini
1½ cups long-grain rice
4 cups chicken stock, room temperature
  (see page 17)
2 cups thinly sliced cabbage
1 cup bean sprouts

2 cups broccoli florets, blanched
1 roasted red pepper, cut into thin
  matchstick strips (see page 8)
salt and freshly ground pepper to taste
sesame oil and tahini to taste
hot chile oil to taste, optional
3 scallions, thinly sliced, for garnish
½ cup sliced almonds, toasted (see
  page 8), for garnish

Heat sesame oil in a small sauté pan over medium heat and sauté onion and garlic until wilted. Add tahini and mix well. Spray a rice cooker with nonstick cooking spray. Add onion mixture and rice. Pour in chicken stock. Cover cooker. Cook according to manufacturer's instructions until rice cooker turns off. Transfer cooked rice to a bowl and add cabbage, bean sprouts, broccoli and roasted pepper. Add salt and pepper and taste for seasonings. Add more sesame oil and tahini if desired. Stir in chile oil, if using. Garnish with scallions and almonds. Serve at room temperature.

BLACK BEAN CONFETTI SALAD

Here is a salad to tempt your winter appetite. The purple onions and bright yellow corn kernels are combined with cooked white rice, pimientos and cilantro. The black beans provide a nutritious, succulent and dramatic complement. You can used canned beans or cook them yourself. You can also add ½-1 lb. of cooked shrimp just before serving.

2 cups cooked black beans
1 cup cooked corn kernels
2 cups cooked white rice (see page 10)
1 cup chopped purple onion
1 cup finely diced pimiento or red bell
   pepper
1 tbs. cumin seeds, toasted and ground
   (see page 9)

3 cloves garlic, minced
½ cup chopped fresh cilantro
6 tbs. olive oil
1 tbs. fresh lemon juice
¼ cup balsamic vinegar
1 tsp. salt
freshly ground pepper to taste

Combine beans with remaining ingredients. This salad is best served at room temperature. It can also be made ahead of time, chilled, and brought to room temperature before serving.

CHICKEN AIOLI RISOTTO SALAD

Servings: 8

Here is another reason to make extra risotto, which adds a creamy, particularly luscious flavor with the toasted hazelnuts. You can substitute any meat or poultry.

1 cup mayonnaise thinned with 1/4 cup chicken stock or white wine
2 cloves garlic, pressed or minced
2 lb. uncooked chicken breast, cut into large dice
salt and freshly ground pepper
2 tbs. olive oil
3-4 cloves garlic, minced

4 cups cooked risotto (see pages 13-23)
1 small red onion, halved, thinly sliced
1 bunch scallions, white and green parts, chopped
1/2 lb. blanched snow peas, cut into thin strips
additional salt and pepper, optional

Mix mayonnaise mixture with 2 cloves garlic to create aioli (garlic mayonnaise). The mayonnaise mixture should be thin enough so that it does not cause the salad to settle into clumps. Set aside. Toss diced chicken with salt, pepper, olive oil and 3 cloves garlic. Sauté chicken in a nonstick sauté pan over medium-high heat for 5 minutes, or until cooked through. Remove chicken from pan and combine with remaining ingredients and aioli. Adjust for seasonings and add more garlic, salt and pepper, if desired.

CORN, RICE AND MUSHROOM MEDLEY

Servings: 6

Here is a colorful salad to serve hot or at room temperature. Although it stands very well alone, it can also serve as a flavorful side dish with fish or poultry.

2 tbs. butter
2 tbs. olive oil
2 cloves garlic, minced
1½ cups sliced leeks, white part only
1 tbs. cumin seeds, toasted and ground
  (see page 9)
2 cups cooked corn kernels
2 cups cooked long-grain rice (see page
  10)

2 cups diced red or orange bell pepper
8-10 dried shiitake mushrooms,
  reconstituted (see page 7)
1 cup chopped purple onion
salt and freshly ground pepper to taste
6 tbs. *Vinaigrette* with 1 additional tbs.
  Dijon mustard (see page 95)
1 cup chopped fresh cilantro
1 tbs. yellow mustard seeds, optional

Melt butter with oil and sauté garlic and leeks over medium heat until soft. Add cumin, corn, rice and bell pepper. Slice mushrooms into thin strips and add to pan. Cook for 3 to 4 minutes to blend flavors. Pour ingredients into a large bowl and add chopped onion. Add salt and pepper. Add mustard vinaigrette and marinate salad for 20 to 30 minutes. Fold in chopped cilantro and mustard seeds, if using, just before serving. To serve hot, add onion, seasonings and vinaigrette just before serving.

FENNEL, MUSHROOM AND TOMATO RICE SALAD

This colorful salad consists of bright yellow Cuban rice mixed with fresh mushrooms that have been marinated in a strong vinaigrette. It is then perfumed with fresh cilantro and augmented with crunchy fresh fennel and other vegetables. Serve it at room temperature, or even slightly warm.

1 tbs. Dijon mustard
1 tsp. dried thyme
1 cup *Vinaigrette*, follows
8 oz. fresh white mushrooms, sliced
1 cup fresh fennel, cut into thin matchstick strips
1/2 cup roasted red pepper strips (see page 8)
2 medium tomatoes, peeled, seeded and diced
1 medium zucchini, skin on, cut into thin matchstick strips
3 cups warm *Cuban Rice*, page 122
3 tbs. chopped cilantro leaves
2 scallions, white and green parts, thinly sliced
salt and freshly ground pepper to taste
spinach leaves
fennel leaves for garnish

Add mustard and thyme to vinaigrette and mix well. In ½ cup of the vinaigrette, marinate mushroom slices for at least 1 hour. Add marinated mushrooms, fennel, roasted red pepper, tomatoes and zucchini to warm rice. Add cilantro, scallions, salt and pepper. Add remaining *Vinaigrette* and taste for seasoning. Spread a few spinach leaves on the bottom of each plate, and mound rice salad on top. Garnish with fennel leaves.

VARIATION
If you prefer a little heat in your salad, add 1 tsp. red pepper flakes or ½ tsp. chile oil to *Vinaigrette.*

VINAIGRETTE
To vary the flavor, any dried or fresh herbs can be added.

1 tsp. dried mustard, or 2 tsp. Dijon
   mustard
¼ cup olive oil

1 tbs. red or white wine vinegar
2 tsp. lemon juice
salt and freshly ground pepper to taste

Place all ingredients in a jar with a tight-fitting lid, and shake vigorously. The result should be emulsified, and look a little cloudy.

POACHED MUSSEL SALAD

Servings: 8-10 as first course; 4-6 as entrée

This salad is best made and eaten the same day, as the mussels lose flavor and their texture becomes a bit rubbery when cooked too far in advance. You can substitute clams or shrimp for the mussels.

2 lb. mussels in the shell
2 cups dry white wine (Chablis or Chardonnay is ideal)
5-6 peppercorns
3-4 bay leaves
1 cup chopped celery with leaves
½ Spanish onion, diced
3 tbs. olive oil
2 cups basmati rice
dry white wine and water
about 10 sun-dried tomatoes, chopped
½ cup chopped fresh basil
½ cup chopped fresh thyme
5 cloves garlic, finely chopped
6 scallions, white and green parts, chopped
1 bunch cilantro, chopped
6 tbs. olive oil
salt and freshly ground pepper to taste

Clean mussels by scrubbing with a stiff brush. Remove beards, and place mussels in cold water to cover until all are cleaned. Drain mussels and transfer to a large pot with 2 cups wine, peppercorns, bay leaves and celery. Cover with a tight-fitting lid and cook mussels over high heat until they open, about 8 minutes. Strain liquid through cheesecloth, being careful not to allow any sand to seep through. Set aside poaching liquid. Remove mussels from shells and set aside. Discard shells.

In a 2-quart pot with a tight-fitting lid, sauté onion in 3 tbs. olive oil. Add rice and stir to coat all grains with oil. Measure strained poaching liquid and (reserving 1/4 cup of the liquid for the sauce) add additional white wine and water in equal proportions to bring measure to 4 cups liquid. Heat liquid to a simmer and add to rice. Bring rice mixture to a boil, cover and lower heat to simmer for 25 minutes. When done, spread rice on a baking sheet to cool. Combine sun-dried tomatoes with cooled rice, basil, thyme, garlic, scallions and cilantro. Add mussels, reserved poaching liquid, 6 tbs. olive oil, salt and pepper. Mix well. This is best served at room temperature.

CHICKEN SOUP WITH PRUNES, RICE AND GARBANZO BEANS

Servings: 6-8

This is really more of a stew than a soup. Since it is quite filling, it needs nothing more than some good rye bread and butter as an accompaniment. A green salad with a mustard vinaigrette, a selection of cheeses, and/or a simple fresh fruit dessert would complete the meal.

3 lb. chicken, whole or parts
1 tsp. salt
4-5 peppercorns
2 carrots, each cut into 4 pieces
2 stalks celery, with leaves, each cut
    into 4 pieces
1 large onion, skin on, root end removed
1 bay leaf
½ lemon, including peel
8 cups water
1 tsp. salt
¼ tsp. freshly ground pepper

⅓ cup butter, margarine or vegetable oil
½ cup chopped onion
1 clove garlic, minced
1 tbs. cumin seeds, toasted and ground
    (see page 9)
1 tbs. dried oregano
¾ cup long-grain rice
1 cup canned garbanzo beans, rinsed
    and drained
1½ cups pitted prunes
¼ cup chopped fresh dill for garnish

Make chicken stock by combining chicken or chicken parts with salt, peppercorns, carrots, celery, whole onion, bay leaf, lemon, water, salt and pepper. Bring to a boil, reduce heat and simmer until tender, about 2 hours. Skim any foam that rises to the top. Strain stock and remove chicken meat from bones. Tear meat into bite-sized pieces. Set aside carrots and chicken meat. Place stock in the refrigerator for a few hours; skim off fat. (Stock can be made a day ahead.)

Melt butter in a 3- or 4-quart heavy pot and sauté chopped onion over medium heat until light brown. Add garlic, cumin and oregano. Add rice and stir for 1 to 2 minutes. Add stock and simmer for 20 minutes. Dice carrots and add to stock with garbanzo beans and prunes. Cook for 20 minutes. Taste and adjust seasonings if necessary. Add chicken meat and cook for 5 minutes. Pour into warm soup bowls and sprinkle with dill.

CREAMY BROCCOLI HAZELNUT SOUP

Servings: 8-10

This soup is good hot or cold. The traditional role of potatoes as part of the soup's base is replaced by rice, resulting in a creamier texture. Make lots of it when broccoli is plentiful, as it freezes beautifully. To save freezer space, you could just prepare the puree itself, and add the chicken stock and cream at a later time. Add more or less rice, depending on the size of broccoli you have used. The desired thickness of the soup is up to you, but I prefer a bisque-like consistency that will coat a spoon.

2 tbs. butter
1 medium onion, sliced
1 bunch leeks, white part only, cleaned
   and sliced
3 cloves garlic, minced
1 tbs. dried thyme
2 bunches broccoli, peeled and chopped
1/2 tsp. salt
freshly ground pepper to taste

4 cups chicken stock (see page 17)
2 cups cooked short- or medium-grain
   white rice (see page 10)
3 tbs. chopped fresh thyme
1 cup half-and-half, heavy cream or
   whole milk
1/4 tsp. grated nutmeg, optional
1 cup hazelnuts, roasted and chopped
   (see page 8), for garnish

Melt butter in a 4-quart saucepan. Over medium heat, sauté onion, leeks and garlic until soft. Add dried thyme and chopped broccoli. Reduce heat to low, cover pot and continue to cook until broccoli is soft, about 10 minutes, depending on size of broccoli pieces. Add salt and pepper and some chicken stock, if ingredients are too dry. When broccoli is tender, add cooked rice. Cook mixture for 5 minutes. Cool broccoli-rice mixture and puree with a blender or food processor, leaving some small chunks. Return mixture to pot and add fresh thyme, chicken stock and half-and-half. Add nutmeg, if using; be careful, as nutmeg has a tendency to overpower other flavors. Taste and adjust seasonings if necessary. Serve hot, garnished with hazelnuts.

CREAMY OYSTER AND SCALLOP SOUP

Servings: 6-8

Onions, leeks and shallots, slowly caramelized in butter, are supplemented with rice and enriched with fish stock, cream and dry sherry. Not a soup for every day, for sure. But for that extra-special dining experience, this is a sure winner. The oysters and scallops are added just before serving, and the soup is further garnished with a sprinkling of chopped chives.

1 tbs. butter
1 large sweet onion, thinly sliced
2 leeks, white part only, cleaned and
    sliced
3 shallots, peeled and chopped
2 cloves garlic, minced
1 cup short-grain white rice
1/2 tsp. dried oregano
1/2 tsp. dried sage

1/2 tsp. dried tarragon
4 cups hot fish stock (see page 16)
3/4 cup heavy cream
salt and freshly ground pepper to taste
1/2 cup dry sherry
18-30 shucked oysters with their juice
24-36 bay scallops
2 tbs. chopped fresh chives

Heat butter in a heavy 3- or 4-quart pot over medium heat. Add onion, leeks, shallots and garlic. Reduce heat to low and sauté very slowly, stirring frequently and scraping the bottom of the pan often, until quite limp and almost caramelized. Add more butter if necessary. Do not burn. Add rice, oregano, sage and tarragon. Mix well. Cover and continue to cook over low heat for about 20 minutes. Check every 5 minutes or so to make sure that there is enough moisture to keep mixture from scorching; add some of the fish stock, if mixture seems to dry. Add ½ of the fish stock, and cook for 10 minutes, covered. Cool mixture, and when cool enough, puree with a blender or food processor in small batches until smooth. Return mixture to pot and add remaining fish stock and cream. Taste for seasoning and add salt and freshly ground pepper. Add sherry. Strain oysters and add their juice to soup. Keep soup at a low simmer, and add oysters and scallops about 5 minutes before serving. Ladle into warm soup bowls and sprinkle with chopped chives.

CUCUMBER RICE SOUP

This cold soup can be the base for many other cold soups, and serves as a foil for bits of leftover vegetables, or even fruit. It is relatively low in calories and superbly refreshing.

3 English (hothouse) cucumbers, peeled and cut into chunks
1 sweet onion, cut into chunks
1 cup chopped fresh dill
3-4 whole scallions, cut into 1-inch pieces
1 qt. buttermilk
1 cup low-fat milk
3 cloves garlic, minced, or more
2 tbs. cumin seeds, toasted and ground (see page 9)
1 cup cooked short- or medium-grain white rice (see page 10)
1 tsp. salt
yogurt or sour cream for garnish
fresh dill sprigs for garnish

Place cucumbers and onion in a food processor workbowl, and process slightly. Add dill, scallions and garlic, and process again, leaving some small pieces for texture. Combine mixture with remaining ingredients, and serve very cold. Garnish with a spoonful of yogurt or sour cream and a sprig of dill.

VARIATIONS

- Omit ½ of the cucumbers and add cooked leftover vegetables, such as fresh spinach, Swiss chard, and even chopped cooked beets.
- For fruit soup lovers, omit onions, garlic and cumin. Add 2 cups cherry puree and 1 tbs. lemon peel.
- Substitute cilantro for the dill. Substitute ground fennel seed, curry powder or ground cardamom seeds for the cumin.

HOMINY RISOTTO SOUP

Servings: 6-8

*Hominy is dried corn that has been soaked in water with lime or lye. This causes the kernels to swell and become loose from their hulls. It is a process that imparts a very special smoky flavor to the grain. After it is dried it can be stored for a long period of time. The Native Americans gave hominy to the early American colonists, which kept them from starving during the harsh winters. This combination of hominy and rice is both nourishing and unusual. Garnish it with a swirl of **Roasted Red Pepper Sauce**, and it will taste spectacular and look elegant.*

1½ cups dried hominy, soaked for 12
    hours in water
water to cover
2 tbs. butter
1 tbs. olive oil
2 leeks, white part only, thinly sliced
½ onion, minced
2 cloves garlic, minced
1 tbs. cumin seeds, ground and toasted
    (see page 9)

1 cup Arborio rice
3 cups simmering chicken stock, or
    more if needed (see page 17)
2 cups corn kernels, fresh or frozen
2 cups canned creamed corn
1 tsp. salt
freshly ground pepper to taste
Roasted Red Pepper Sauce, page 85, for
    garnish

Drain hominy and rinse in water. In a medium saucepan, cover hominy with water and bring to a boil. Reduce heat to low and simmer for 45 minutes. Drain hominy, reserving 1 cup of the cooking water; set aside. Heat butter and oil in a 3-quart saucepan over medium heat. Add leeks, onion and garlic and sauté for 3 to 4 minutes, until soft, but not brown. Add cumin and mix well. Add rice and stir to coat all grains with fat. Add 1 cup of the hot chicken stock. Keep stirring, and as rice absorbs stock, add another cup. Continue in this manner until all stock is absorbed. Add fresh corn kernels, creamed corn and hominy with 1 cup reserved cooking water. Cook soup over low heat. Do not let it reduce to such a thick state that it will scorch. Add more chicken stock, if necessary. When hominy is fully cooked, in about 30 to 45 minutes, add salt and pepper. Taste for seasoning and adjust, if necessary. Cool soup and puree in batches, leaving about ⅓ unpureed. Return to low heat, stirring frequently, until hot. Serve garnished with *Roasted Red Pepper Sauce*.

VARIATION

If you really like spicy food, add hot jalapeño sauce to taste just before serving.

SPINACH RICE SOUP WITH PROSCIUTTO

Servings: 6-8

This is almost a risotto dish in reverse. We start with a double-strength broth and add the vegetables, rice and prosciutto. An intensely flavored broth is important to the success of this soup. Fresh spinach and thin strips of prosciutto ham and a garnish of omelet shreds add nourishment and pizzazz.

1 lb. beef chuck meat
1 beef marrow bone
6 cups beef stock (see page 18)
½ cup chopped celery
½ cup chopped carrots
½ cup chopped onion
1 tsp. salt
4 peppercorns
1 bay leaf
water to cover
2 tbs. butter

1 tbs. olive oil
1 cup sliced leeks, white part only
½ cup minced onion
¾ cup Arborio rice
1 lb. fresh spinach, tough center ribs
    removed, chopped
1 tsp. vegetable oil
2 eggs, beaten with pinch salt and pepper
6 thin slices prosciutto
salt and freshly ground pepper to taste
grated Reggiano Parmesan cheese

Wrap meat and bone in cheesecloth that has been rinsed in cold water, to keep any fat particles from escaping into the soup. In a 6- to 8-quart pot, place beef broth, beef and bone, celery, carrots, onion, salt, peppercorns and bay leaf. Add water to cover, and bring to a boil over high heat. Reduce heat to medium and cook for 1½ hours. If liquid evaporates too quickly, place a lid askew on pot to prevent all steam from escaping.

While broth is cooking, melt butter and olive oil in a 2-quart saucepan over medium heat. Add leeks and onion and sauté until wilted. Add rice and stir for 2 minutes. Add chopped spinach, cover pan and turn off heat. Set aside. Heat a small sauté pan and add vegetable oil. Pour in beaten eggs, and using a spoon or spatula, draw edges of egg in as it becomes cooked. At the same time, tilt pan to allow liquid eggs to settle around edge of pan. When firm, turn off heat and turn egg out on a wooden board to cool. Cut egg into thin strips, about ¼-inch wide. Set aside. Cut thin slices of prosciutto into strips about the same size. When broth is done, strain through fine cheesecloth and return to pot. Adjust seasoning if necessary. Add spinach-rice mixture and cook for 15 to 20 minutes, or until rice is just slightly firm in the center. Add egg and prosciutto strips. Serve in warmed soup bowls with grated Parmesan cheese on the side.

WILD MUSHROOM BROWN RICE SOUP

Servings: 8-10

This is an elegant version of good old mushroom barley soup. Porcini mushrooms are also called cepes. The dried version of these mushrooms is preferred over the fresh, as the reconstituting liquid is what makes this soup so special. If you cannot find porcini, use any dried mushrooms.

2 oz. dried porcini mushrooms, reconstituted (see page 7)
2 lb. boneless chuck
1 beef soup bone
1 large onion, diced
1 leek, white and green parts, cleaned, cut into thin matchstick strips
3 carrots, diced
1 lb. potatoes, peeled and diced
3 qt. water
1 large tomato, peeled, seeded and chopped
1 cup brown rice
salt and freshly ground pepper to taste

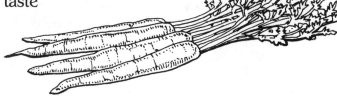

Strain liquid in which mushrooms have soaked through a cheesecloth and reserve. Tie beef and bone in cheesecloth that has been rinsed in cold water, to keep any loose bits of fat from floating into soup. Spray a 4-quart pot with nonstick vegetable spray, and sauté diced onion and leek over medium heat until slightly wilted. Add strained mushroom liquid, mushrooms, carrots and potatoes. Simmer for 2 minutes to meld flavors. Add 3 quarts water, beef and bone in cheesecloth, and tomato. Bring to a boil and skim off any foam that rises to the surface. Reduce heat and simmer for 15 minutes, removing any additional foam. Add brown rice, salt and pepper. Return to a boil. Reduce heat and simmer for at least 2 hours, and up to 3 hours. Remove cheesecloth with beef and bone from liquid. Untie bundle and cool. Cut meat into bite-sized pieces, removing any fat or gristle, discard soup bone and return meat to pot. Taste for seasonings and adjust if necessary.

VARIATION

For added flavor, add 1 tbs. medium-dry Madeira or dry sherry to each bowl of soup before serving.

HERBED TOMATO RICE SOUP

Servings: 8

Here is a great summertime treat, when tomatoes are ripe and luscious. Serve it chilled, garnished with yogurt or sour cream and a sprig of dill. You can also add hot sauce to taste, bringing a little "zing" to the dish. However, a steaming bowl of this soup on a frosty winter day is also totally satisfying. When served with an old-fashioned tuna fish sandwich on white bread, it's instant nostalgia for some of us!

1 large Spanish onion, diced
1 green bell pepper, diced
1 stalk celery, chopped
3 cloves garlic, minced
3 tbs. olive oil
1 tsp. dried basil, or more to taste
1 tsp. dried oregano, or more to taste

1 tsp. dried thyme, or more to taste
6 cups chicken stock
4 cups chopped peeled tomatoes (fresh or canned)
2 cups cooked white rice, any size grain (see page 10)
salt and freshly ground pepper to taste

In a 2- to 3-quart pot over medium heat, sauté onion, pepper, celery and garlic in olive oil until soft. Add dried herbs and sauté for 30 seconds. Add chicken stock, tomatoes and cooked rice. Add salt and pepper.

SIDE DISHES

INDONESIAN RICE

This is a marvelous mixture of rice, vegetables and spices, topped with chopped scallions and strips of egg and ham. It is really an Indonesian version of fried rice, although I find it more exotic and interesting. Like fried rice, this basic recipe can be elaborated upon to your heart's content. This reheats very well from room temperature, covered, in a 350° oven for 20 minutes, or on top of the stove.

2 cups long-grain rice
½ tsp. salt, optional
3 cups water
½ cup dried onion flakes
1 cup water
1 tbs. curry powder
½ tbs. cumin seeds, toasted and ground
    (see page 9)
1 tsp. turmeric
2 tbs. vegetable oil
1 large sweet onion, thinly sliced

2-3 cloves garlic, minced
salt and freshly ground pepper to taste
1 tsp. minced fresh chile pepper
1 large egg
1 tbs. water
2 tsp. vegetable oil
2 oz. boiled ham, cut into slivers, for
    garnish
2 whole scallions, sliced into rings, for
    garnish

Place rice in a 2-quart pot. Add salt, if using, and 3 cups water. Bring to a rapid boil, cover, and turn heat down to produce a slight simmer. Cook for 20 minutes. Do not remove lid. Remove from heat and allow rice to steam, covered, for 20 minutes. While rice is cooking, reconstitute onion flakes with 1 cup water in a small pot. Bring water to a boil, turn heat off, and stir for a few minutes. Combine curry powder, cumin and turmeric and set aside. Heat 2 tbs. vegetable oil in a large sauté pan. Add sliced onion and minced garlic. Cook over medium heat until onion is wilted and add reconstituted onion. Sauté for 1 minute. Add cooked rice and mix thoroughly into sautéed ingredients. Add salt, pepper and fresh chile pepper, if using. Taste for seasonings and adjust if necessary.

Break egg into a small bowl, add 1 tbs. water and beat until well combined. Heat a small frying or omelet pan with 2 tsp. oil. When very hot (a drop of water should bounce), pour beaten egg into pan. Roll pan around gently to cover hot surface with egg. Return to burner and continuously spoon uncooked portion of egg from edges into the middle. When dry, turn off heat and cover for 1 minute. Slide onto a cutting board, cut into quarters and then into shreds about $1/8$-inch wide. Set aside. Pile rice mixture into a serving dish and garnish with cooked egg, ham and scallions. Garnishing ingredients should be at room temperature. If you make rice 1 to 2 days ahead, garnish just before serving.

VARIATION
For a one-dish meal, add shrimp, diced cooked pork, peas or other items.

RISOTTO-STUFFED ONIONS

Servings: 6

The combination of rice and onions has been the backbone of many interesting and classic recipes. In this side dish or appetizer, sweet onions are braised and stuffed with a mixture of risotto and shredded carrots. The onion becomes almost caramelized, and is juicy and appetizing. Select firm, unblemished, unsprouted onions.

6 large sweet onions
water to cover
1 tbs. olive oil
2 tsp. dried thyme
2 tbs. grated ginger root
1 cup shredded carrots
½ tsp. salt
freshly ground pepper to taste
½ cup Madeira or Marsala wine, optional
2 cups risotto (see pages 13-23)
1 cup beef or chicken stock (see page 18, 17)
¼ cup grated Reggiano Parmesan cheese
½ cup fresh or dried breadcrumbs
2 tbs. butter

In a large saucepan, place onions and cover with water. Bring to a boil, lower heat and simmer for 10 minutes. Remove onions and plunge into cold water. Heat oven to 375°. Cut a slice from the bottom and top of each onion. With a spoon, hollow out the center of each onion, leaving a ¼-inch shell on all sides and bottom. Chop onion centers.

Heat olive oil over medium heat and sauté onion centers with dried thyme and ginger for about 1 minute. Add carrots and sauté for 1 minute. Taste for seasoning and add salt and pepper. Add 2 tbs. of the Marsala. Add vegetable mixture to risotto and fill onion shells. Set shells in a casserole just large enough to hold them upright. Mix grated Parmesan cheese with breadcrumbs; sprinkle over stuffed onions. Dot with butter and pour remaining wine and stock around bottoms of onions. Cover loosely with foil and roast until tender, about 30 minutes, removing foil after the first 15 minutes. Baste from time to time to keep onions moist.

FILLED RICE BALLS

Yield: 8-10

This recipe obviously has evolved since the first person determined that leftover rice was a good vehicle to combine with other foods.

2 tbs. diced onion
2 tsp. olive oil
3 cups cooked risotto (see pages 13-23)
2 tbs. chopped fresh flat-leaf parsley
2 eggs, beaten
1/2 cup grated Reggiano Parmesan cheese

salt and freshly ground pepper to taste
4 oz. mozzarella cheese, cut into small cubes
1/2 cup dried breadcrumbs
vegetable oil

In a small sauté pan, sauté onion in olive oil over medium heat until soft. In a bowl, combined sautéed onion, risotto, parsley, eggs, cheese, salt and pepper and stir until well mixed. Form mixture, about 1/4 cup at a time, into football or egg shapes. Push 2 cubes of the mozzarella cheese into each shape and reform. Coat with breadcrumbs. Chill for at least 1 hour. Fill a 12-inch sauté pan with vegetable oil to a depth of 1 inch and heat until hot but not smoking. Fry rice balls, turning until all sides are brown. Drain well on paper towels.

VARIATION

Brush rice balls with oil and bake in a 375° oven for about 20 minutes, turning once, until brown. Serve warm or hot.

SAUCY BEANS AND RICE

When in New Orleans, be sure to find a restaurant or (if you are lucky) get invited to a dinner which features this regional specialty.

2½ lb. dried red kidney beans, soaked
    overnight in water to cover
1 large bone from a baked ham, cut
    into pieces
1½ cups chopped baked ham
5 cloves garlic, minced
1 small green bell pepper, chopped
3 cups diced Spanish onions
½ cup chopped scallions
½ cup chopped fresh flat-leaf parsley

12 oz. salt pork, cut into 3 or 4 pieces
1 tbs. black peppercorns
3 bay leaves, crushed
1 cup fresh thyme, or 2 tbs. dried
1 crushed dried hot red pepper
½ cup chopped fresh basil, or 1 tbs. dried
water to cover
6 cups cooked medium-grain white rice
chopped flat-leaf parsley and diced
    onion for garnish, optional

Rinse and drain beans. Place all ingredients, except rice and garnishes, in a heavy 8-quart pot. Bring to a boil, reduce heat to low and cover tightly. Cook for about 4 hours. Stir deeply occasionally to help prevent sticking to the bottom. Add more water if necessary. Remove salt pork and ham bone and discard. Serve beans over cooked rice. Garnish with chopped parsley and diced onion if desired.

BROWN RICE AND RISOTTO TIMBALES

You can serve rice as a side dish plopped on the plate, arranged nicely in a mound, or finicky elegant as in a timbale. Serve these elegant timbales with a simple poached boneless chicken breast or grilled salmon, garnished with diced roasted red pepper.

2 tbs. olive oil
1 clove garlic, minced
3 tbs. chopped shallots
½ tsp. rubbed sage
2 cups cooked risotto (see pages 13-23)

2 cups cooked brown rice (see page 10)
3 tbs. chopped fresh chives
1-2 steamed carrots
1 tbs. soft butter for greasing molds

Heat oven to 350°. Heat olive oil in a 2-quart sauté pan over medium heat. Add garlic and shallots and cook for 3 to 4 minutes until soft. Add sage and heat for 1 minute. Add cooked risotto and brown rice and stir to blend all ingredients. Transfer rice mixture to a large bowl and stir in chives. Cut steamed carrots into ¼-inch-thick rounds. Grease six to eight 2- to 4-ounce timbales, pyrex cups or soufflé cups. Arrange carrot rounds on the bottom of each mold in an overlapping pattern. Pack cooled rice mixture into each mold, being careful not to move carrot slices. Place molds in a baking dish containing about ½-inch of boiling water. Bake for about 10 minutes. Remove cups from baking pan with a hot pad, wipe dry and unmold on individual plates. Be careful that no stray liquid leaks from the mold, resulting in a messy plate.

EGGPLANT ATHENA

Follow the directions carefully for removing moisture from the eggplant, so it will be ready to absorb flavors. The difference in taking this step will amaze you.

2 large eggplants, peeled and cut into
  1/2-inch cubes
1 tbs. salt
3 tbs. olive oil
1 large sweet onion, minced
4 cloves garlic, minced
1 cup dried breadcrumbs
1/2 cup drained canned or fresh tomatoes,
  peeled and chopped

1/2 tsp. dried red pepper flakes
1 tbs. cumin seeds, roasted and ground
  (see page 9)
1 tbs. dried oregano
3 tbs. chopped fresh oregano
salt and freshly ground pepper to taste
1 cup long-grain white rice
3 cups chicken stock (see page 17)
1 cup grated Romano or kashkeval cheese

Heat oven to 375°. Place diced eggplant in a colander and sprinkle with 1 tbs. salt. Let it sit for 20 minutes and squeeze dry in a clean towel. Heat olive oil in a 3-quart ovenproof casserole over medium heat. Sauté onion and garlic until soft. In a bowl, toss breadcrumbs with eggplant. Add to casserole and sauté until light brown. Add tomatoes, red pepper flakes, cumin, dried and fresh oregano, salt and pepper. Simmer over low heat for 5 minutes. Mix in rice and chicken stock, cover and bake for 20 minutes. Remove cover and spread with grated cheese. Bake for 20 minutes.

CUBAN RICE

Achiote is a bright orange powder from the seed of the annatto tree. Although the flavor is elusive, the color is vibrant, and I like to use spices and herbs to match its vibrancy. It's available as seed or powder in most Latin American, Spanish and East Indian markets. Serve this as a side dish with fish or fowl, or top it with something grilled or sautéed for a brilliant first course or entrée.

2 tbs. vegetable oil
1 tbs. butter
1/2 onion, minced
2 cloves garlic, minced
2 tsp. cumin seeds, toasted and ground
  (see page 9)
2 tsp. dried oregano

2 cups long-grain rice
4 1/2 cups fish, beef or vegetable stock
  (see pages 16-18)
1 tsp. ground achiote seed
1 tsp. salt, or more to taste
3 tbs. chopped cilantro
freshly ground pepper to taste

Spray a rice cooker with nonstick cooking spray. Heat vegetable oil and butter in uncovered rice cooker. Add onion and garlic and sauté until soft. Add cumin and oregano; stir. Add rice, turning to combine ingredients evenly. Add stock, ground achiote and salt. Cover cooker, and cook according to the manufacturer's instructions, or until it turns off. When rice is done, add cilantro. Taste for seasoning and add pepper, and more salt, if desired.

CUMIN RIZCOUS

Rizcous is a fairly new product, made from brown rice that is cooked, dehydrated, and reformed into little grain-like shapes that cook very quickly. Rizcous is a great adjunct to that impulsive last-minute invitation, as it cooks quickly and can be dressed up elegantly. Serve rizcous with grilled **Monkfish Saté,** *page 133.*

2 tbs. olive oil, or more to taste
½ large sweet onion, chopped
2 tbs. cumin seeds, toasted and ground
   (see page 9)
3½ cups chicken stock (see page 17)

2 cups rizcous
½ tsp. salt
¼ cup toasted pine nuts (see page 8),
   optional

Heat oil in a 1-quart saucepan over medium heat. Sauté onion until golden. Add cumin and mix well to coat onion. Add chicken stock, rizcous and salt. Bring to a boil, cover, reduce heat to low and cook for 5 minutes. Turn off heat and steam, covered, for 3 to 4 minutes. Fluff with a fork and taste for seasoning. Add more olive oil, if desired. Sprinkle with pine nuts, if using, just before serving.

VARIATIONS

Try other seasonings, such as minced garlic, chopped fresh chives, or grated orange or lemon peel. Add chopped fresh cilantro or, at the last steaming, add ½ cup chopped dried apricots. Rizcous goes very well with lamb or chicken.

BEANS AND RICE KIEV

There is a marriage of rice and beans in most cultures. The beans may vary, but rice remains constant. The combination is nutritious, inexpensive and always satisfying. Here is a recipe that proves my point. Arborio rice works well in this dish as it holds its firmness during the long cooking period, but try it with brown rice, too.

1 large onion, sliced
2 tbs. vegetable oil
1 tbs. flour
1 clove garlic, minced
salt and coarsely ground pepper
2 lb. center cut beef chuck roast

1 lb. dried lima beans, washed
paprika
salt and freshly ground pepper to taste
3 cups uncooked Arborio rice
water

Heat oven to 350°. In a 6-quart heavy pot over medium heat, sauté onion in oil until light brown. Remove onion and set aside. Turn heat to medium-high. Rub flour, garlic, salt and pepper on all sides of meat and sear on all sides until dark brown. Return onion to pot with lima beans. Sprinkle paprika, salt and pepper over beans and meat. Add Arborio rice. Cover with water. Cover tightly and bake until beans have absorbed most of the water and rice is cooked, about 2 to 3 hours. To serve, cut meat into slices or chunks, arrange on individual plates and cover with beans and thick sauce.

BLACK-EYED PEAS AND RICE

Servings: 6-8

This dish resembles a dish called "Hoppin' John," which is traditionally served in the southern United States on New Year's Day to ensure the eater good luck in the coming year. If chopping the ham hock is difficult, use bits and pieces of cooked baked ham and a ham bone. Black-eyed peas are really beans.

1½ cups dried black-eyed peas, soaked
    overnight in water to cover
1 ham hock, chopped
1 tsp. red pepper flakes
½ large Spanish onion, chopped
½ tsp. freshly ground pepper

1½ cups long-grain rice
3 cups cold water
2 tbs. vegetable oil
½ cup chopped fresh flat-leaf parsley
salt to taste, optional

Rinse and drain peas. In a heavy 4-quart pot, combine peas with ham, pepper flakes, onion and pepper. Cook over low heat, covered, until peas are tender. Check from time to time and add more water if necessary. Cook until peas are tender and all water has been absorbed. While peas are cooking, place rice in a 2-quart pot with 3 cups cold water and 2 tbs. oil. Bring to a boil, cover and reduce heat. Simmer for 20 minutes, remove pot from heat and steam rice, covered, for 20 minutes. Mix rice thoroughly with cooked peas and garnish with parsley. Add salt if desired.

MIXED RICE CASSEROLE

Servings: 6-8

This is an uncomplicated casserole of wild, brown short-grain and white long-grain rice. Its simplicity does not detract from its subtle, yet satisfying, taste, and it complements almost any entrée. It also stands very well by itself, the shiitake mushrooms providing a meaty texture, and the combination of rices an interesting crunch. Use stock to complement your entrée. Although wild rice is not a true rice, but a marsh grass, it adds a satisfying nutty texture to this recipe. Wash it in cold water several times and remove any debris that floats to the surface before proceeding with the recipe.

½ cup wild rice
¼ cup short-grain brown rice
¼ cup long-grain white rice
2 oz. dried shiitake mushrooms
1 tbs. olive oil
1 medium yellow onion, diced
3 cloves garlic, minced
1 tbs. dried oregano
1 tbs. dried thyme

1 large can (28 oz.) whole peeled
   tomatoes, coarsely chopped, with juice
½ lb. feta cheese, crumbled
½ tsp. red pepper flakes
2 cups hot chicken, beef or fish stock or
   water (see pages 16-18)
1½ tsp. salt
½ tsp. freshly ground pepper

Soak all rices together in cold water for 1 to 3 hours. Drain when ready to assemble recipe.

Heat oven to 350°. Place dried shiitake mushrooms in a small saucepan, covered with ½-inch water. Bring to a boil and turn off heat. Allow to sit for at least 1 hour. Drain and reserve liquid. Squeeze any remaining liquid from mushrooms and slice into thin strips.

Spray a large sauté pan with nonstick cooking spray and add olive oil. Add onion and garlic and sauté briefly over medium heat. Add mushrooms and sauté for 3 to 4 minutes. Add oregano and thyme and sauté for 1 minute. Add drained rice. Add tomatoes and juice to rice mixture with feta cheese and red pepper flakes. Add hot stock or water, salt and pepper. Place in a casserole dish about 10-x-10-x-2 inches and bake for 1 hour or until liquid is absorbed.

MOORS AND CHRISTIANS (BLACK BEANS AND RICE)

Servings: 8-10

I first tasted this as a soup in a restaurant in Puerto Rico. As a side dish, the beans can be spooned on top of the steaming rice. It's great either way. Black beans are sometimes called turtle beans. Add sliced cooked sausage to make this an entrée.

3 cups black beans, soaked overnight in
    water, rinsed and drained
4 cups water
4 oz. salt pork, chopped
3 tbs. vegetable oil
3 cloves garlic, minced
1 Spanish onion, finely chopped
2 bay leaves, crushed

$\frac{1}{2}$ tsp. freshly ground pepper
hot cooked medium- or long-grain rice
    (see page 10): for soup $\frac{1}{2}$ cup per
    serving; for side dish 1 cup per serving
1 cup chopped fresh cilantro stems and
    leaves
1 cup chopped Spanish onion
hot chicken stock (see page 17), optional

In a heavy 4-quart pot, simmer beans in water until tender, about 2 hours. Add more water if necessary. Sauté salt pork in oil over medium heat until brown. Add garlic, 1 chopped onion, bay leaves and pepper. Sauté until onion is soft. Add to beans and simmer for 20 minutes. For a side dish, spoon beans directly onto rice and pass chopped cilantro and onion. For soup, add hot chicken stock to desired consistency, pour into heated individual bowls and top with chopped cilantro and onion.

JAMAICAN RICE AND PIGEON PEAS

Servings: 6-8

Pigeon peas come from Africa, and are sometimes called "congo" peas. They are about the size of a green pea, and the pods are twisted and fuzzy. This recipe, however, with its chile peppers, is decidedly Jamaican!

3 cups pigeon peas, soaked overnight in water, rinsed and drained
water to cover
½ lb. chopped salt pork
1 medium Spanish onion, diced
3 cloves garlic, minced
1½ cups seeded peeled tomatoes
2-3 bay leaves

½ cup chopped fresh thyme, or 2 tbs. dried
2 small fresh chile peppers, seeds removed, chopped
2½ cups long-grain white rice (see page 10)
4 cups water

In a heavy 4-quart pot, cover peas with water and simmer until almost tender, about 1 hour. Sauté salt pork, diced onion and garlic over medium heat until onion is soft. Add tomatoes, bay leaves, thyme and chile peppers. Drain peas and place in a heavy large pot. Add uncooked rice, tomato-salt pork mixture and 4 cups water. Bring to a boil, cover with a heavy lid, reduce heat and simmer for 25 minutes. Remove from heat, but keep covered for 20 minutes.

SAVORY RISOTTO SOUFFLÉ

Servings: 6

This is an elegant way to use leftover rice. Keep it in mind the next time you make a basic risotto, and cook extra rice to use in this recipe.

1 tbs. olive oil
½ cup diced onion
½ cup chopped leeks, white part only
2 tsp. minced garlic
1 tbs. cumin seeds, toasted and ground
  (see page 9)
½ cup golden raisins
½ cup shredded carrots
salt and pepper to taste
3 tbs. butter or margarine
¼ cup flour
½ cup milk

½ cup chicken stock (see page 17)
5 large eggs, separated
3 cups cooked risotto (see pages 13-23)
½ cup chopped fresh flat-leaf parsley
½ tsp. salt
freshly ground pepper to taste
1 tbs. butter
½ cup fine breadcrumbs
½ tbs. curry powder
½ cup finely grated Reggiano Parmesan
  cheese

Heat oven to 350°. Heat olive oil in a large sauté pan over medium heat, and cook onion, leeks and garlic until soft, but not brown. Add cumin and sauté for 1 minute. Add raisins and carrots. Cook for 5 minutes. Add salt and pepper. Remove from heat and cool. This step can be done ahead.

Melt 3 tbs. butter in a 2-quart saucepan. Slowly whisk in flour. Do not allow mixture to brown. Cook for 3 to 4 minutes, stirring. Slowly add milk and chicken stock, whisking. Mixture will become quite thick. Strain sauce and add about ½ cup to egg yolks and whisk together. With a wooden spoon, stir egg yolk mixture back into saucepan. Remove from heat. Add cooked risotto, chopped parsley, salt and pepper. Beat egg whites to soft peaks.

Rub an 8- or 10-cup soufflé dish with 1 tbs. butter. Combine breadcrumbs, curry powder and grated Parmesan cheese and coat inside of soufflé dish; set aside remaining crumbs. Mix ⅓ of the beaten egg whites with rice-sauce mixture. Fold in remaining beaten egg whites and pour into a 2½- to 3-quart soufflé dish. Sprinkle remaining crumbs over top and bake in the middle of oven for 30 to 40 minutes, until brown and puffed.

ENTRÉES

MONKFISH SATÉ WITH CUMIN RIZCOUS

*Although this entrée is especially good with **Cumin Rizcous**, it goes well with any basic risotto. The marinade can be used with fish or fowl, and can be adjusted for spiciness. Soak wooden skewers in water for 20 minutes before grilling.*

½ cup minced onion
2 cloves garlic, minced
⅓ cup sliced almonds
½ cup soy sauce
1 tbs. curry powder
1 tsp. cumin seeds, toasted and ground
    (see page 9)

1 tsp. finely minced fresh hot chiles, or
    more to taste
¼ cup water
1½ lb. monkfish, cut into 1-inch pieces
1 tbs. vegetable oil
Cumin Rizcous, page 123, or cooked
    risotto (see pages 13-23)

Place onion, garlic and almonds, if using, in a food processor workbowl. Pulse once or twice to blend ingredients. Combine soy sauce, curry, cumin and red pepper paste in a small bowl. Add processed ingredients and water, mixing to blend well. Add monkfish and marinate for at least 1 hour. Heat a grill to hot and brush with vegetable oil. Thread 4 or 5 pieces of fish on each skewer. Grill for about 2 minutes on first side and 1 to 2 minutes on second side. Monkfish will cook very quickly; overcooking results in a tough texture. Serve with *Cumin Rizcous*.

BARCELONA PAELLA

I remember well the first paella I observed in the making, in a kitchen in Barcelona. The aromas are still fresh in my memory, and I can hear the sizzling of the pork ribs. Paella can contain anything you like: poultry (browned first), baby squid, fresh beans, or saffron added to the stock are all authentic touches. With this recipe, I have tried to reproduce what I still think is the best paella ever.

1 lb. fresh cod, cut into 8 pieces
salt and pepper
1 bay leaf
½ medium onion, sliced
1 carrot, sliced
water to cover
¼ cup olive oil
8 pork ribs (country ribs), or 1 lb. chorizo sausage, casing removed, cut into 2-inch pieces
1 large onion, chopped
4 cloves garlic, minced
3 cups Arborio rice
6-8 medium tomatoes, peeled, seeded and chopped

salt
freshly ground pepper to taste
1 cup peas, fresh or frozen
2 cups artichoke hearts, frozen or canned
2 large red bell peppers, roasted (see page 8), cut into strips
16 mussels in shells, washed and scrubbed
8-16 small clams in shells
8 small lobster tails, shell on, cut in half
16 shrimp (21-25 per lb.) in shells
water as needed

In a 2-quart saucepan, place cod, salt, pepper, bay leaf, onion, carrot and water to cover. Cook cod over medium heat, uncovered, until firm, about 5 minutes. Drain and reserve liquid, discard vegetables and set fish aside.

In a paella pan, 14-inch sauté pan or heavy, shallow pan, heat 1 tbs. of the olive oil over medium-high heat and sauté pork ribs until brown on all sides. Remove from pan. Add chopped onions and garlic, and sauté briefly. Add remaining olive oil. Add rice and stir to coat all grains with olive oil. Add tomatoes, salt and pepper. Reheat liquid in which fish was cooked, and add water, if necessary, to make 6 cups liquid. Add liquid to ingredients in paella pan and turn heat to high, stirring frequently. Add pork ribs, reduce heat and simmer for 20 to 25 minutes. Add peas, artichoke hearts and red pepper strips, arranging in a decorative fashion. Cook for 10 minutes. Add mussels, clams, lobster tails, shrimp and partially cooked cod around edge of paella. Simmer for 15 minutes. When rice is done, liquid is entirely absorbed, shellfish are open and lobster tails are cooked through, paella is done. You can cover paella for the last 5 minutes to preserve heat, and force any shellfish to open that may still be tightly closed.

CORN, LOBSTER AND POTATO WHITE PAELLA

This recipe is a compact version of a steamed lobster bucket, and could be called a "white paella." The corn is roasted, which imparts a more intense flavor. The lobster is out of the shell, and the new potatoes are diced and cooked right along with the rice. The creaminess of the cooked risotto is a vehicle which smoothly combines all of these elements, resulting in a delectable repast.

1 cup fresh corn, about 2 ears, precooked for 2-3 minutes
12 clams in shells, optional
12 mussels in shells, optional
5-6 cups hot fish stock (see page 16)
2 tbs. olive oil
½ cup minced sweet onion
2 cloves garlic, minced
2 tsp. Old Bay seasoning
1½ cups diced, peeled new potatoes, ½-inch dice
2 cups Arborio rice
½ tsp. salt
2 cups cooked lobster meat
1 cup sliced scallions, white and green parts

Heat oven to 400°. Spread corn kernels on an oiled baking sheet and roast for 15 to 20 minutes. Check after 10 minutes, and turn over. Corn should become light brown. Remove from oven and set aside. Steam clams and mussels over high heat for 5 minutes with 1 cup of the fish stock in a covered pot. Remove clams and mussels when open and leave in shells; set aside. Discard unopened shells. Strain shellfish cooking liquid through cheesecloth and add to hot fish stock. If you are not continuing with the recipe, refrigerate cooked shellfish.

Heat olive oil in a 4-quart saucepan over medium heat and sauté onions and garlic until soft. Add Old Bay seasoning. Add potatoes and cook for 3 to 4 minutes. Add Arborio rice, stirring to coat grains with oil. Add salt. Add hot fish stock, about 1 cup at a time. As each cup of liquid is absorbed, add the next cup, stirring constantly. When rice grains are still slightly firm in the center, but soft on the outside, *al dente*, add roasted corn, mixing well to distribute evenly. Remove from heat and fold in lobster meat. Sprinkle in sliced scallions. Spoon into warm individual bowls, topping each with 2 clams and 2 mussels, if using.

VARIATION
Add cooked, peeled shrimp just before serving.

KEDGEREE

Servings: 6-8

This dish is of East Indian origin, and usually includes red lentils, available in specialty markets. The more common black or dark green lentils can be substituted. The British added smoked fish and hard-cooked eggs as well as a cream sauce.

2 tbs. butter
1 tbs. vegetable oil
2 tbs. curry powder
¾ cup diced sweet onion
1 cup basmati rice
2 cups fish stock (see page 16)
1 cup dry white wine
½ tsp. salt
½ cup lentils
8-10 oz. smoked bluefish, skinned and boned
1 cup green peas, fresh or frozen
½ cup thinly sliced purple onion
½ tsp. salt
freshly ground pepper to taste
¼ cup sliced almonds, toasted (see page 8), for garnish
6 eggs, poached, or 3 hard-cooked eggs, quartered, for garnish, optional

138 ENTRÉES

Melt butter with oil in a 3-quart saucepan. Add curry powder, and blend for 1 to 2 minutes. Add onion and sauté over medium heat until soft, about 10 minutes. Add rice and stir to coat all grains with fat. Mix fish stock with white wine and add to rice. Bring to a boil, cover and reduce heat. Simmer for 10 minutes. Add lentils and continue to cook for 15 minutes. Break smoked fish into small pieces and add to mixture. Heat briefly. Add peas and purple onion and continue heating until warmed through. Add salt and pepper, taste for seasonings and adjust if necessary. Serve garnished with almonds, and eggs if desired.

VARIATION

To turn this into a cold dish, dissolve 2 tsp. curry powder in ½ cup white wine or fish stock, mix with about ½ cup mayonnaise, and garnish with hard-cooked eggs and chopped scallions. Use any kind of smoked fish that will easily flake. Smoked mackerel, whitefish, or chunk smoked salmon work very well.

RICE VALENCIA, PHILIPPINE-STYLE

Servings: 6-8

I tasted this many times, in many variations, during my years in the Far East. It is really a kind of paella, (except for the coconut milk), and was often served at large parties. As with all multi-ingredient rice dishes, you can add other or subtract any of the vegetables or meats you wish.

2 cups short-grain white rice
2½ cups chicken stock (see page 17) or
    water, or more if needed
1 cup coconut milk, or more if needed
½ tsp. salt
salt and freshly ground pepper to taste
4 lb. chicken, cut into serving pieces
1 lb. boneless pork loin, cut into 2-inch
    cubes
3 cloves garlic, minced
4 oz. spicy sausage, such as chorizo,
    cut into 1-inch pieces
1 tbs. vegetable oil

1 medium onion, coarsely chopped
4 large potatoes, peeled and cut into
    eighths
2 cups drained canned plum tomatoes
1 tsp. paprika
1 cup sliced roasted red bell pepper
    (see page 8)
1 cup frozen green peas
½ cup pimiento-stuffed olives
3 hard-cooked eggs, cut into quarters,
    for garnish

Place rice in a 2-quart pot with chicken stock and coconut milk. Add ½ tsp. salt and bring to a boil. Lower heat and cover. Cook for about 15 minutes at low heat. Remove cover. Rice should be slightly undercooked. Remove rice from pot and set aside. Sprinkle salt and pepper over chicken pieces and pork cubes. Rub with ½ of the minced garlic.

In a 4-to 6-quart heavy pot, brown chicken, pork and sausage pieces in vegetable oil. Remove pieces when brown. Add remaining garlic and chopped onion, and brown slightly. Add potatoes and cook for about 5 minutes. Add tomatoes. Return meats to pan, cover pot and cook over low heat for about 30 minutes, or until meats are tender and potato is cooked through. Add rice, mixing gently to distribute evenly. Sprinkle with paprika, and add more liquid (stock or coconut milk) if pot seems dry. About 15 minutes before serving, stir in red pepper strips, peas and olives. Serve garnished with eggs.

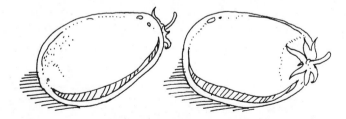

BALKAN CABBAGE ROLLS

These cabbage rolls are reassuringly comforting, and the unusual addition of cinnamon to the filling will pique the most jaded appetite.

1 large cabbage
2 large onions, chopped
6 cloves garlic, minced
2 leeks, white part only, chopped
6 oz. slab bacon, cut into cubes
1½ cups chopped peeled, seeded plum
    tomatoes
1 cup chopped fresh flat-leaf parsley
¾ lb. ground veal
¾ lb. ground pork

¾ lb. ground beef
1 cup long-grain white rice
1 tsp. cinnamon
1 tsp. ground nutmeg
1 tbs. salt
freshly ground pepper to taste
2 cups sauerkraut, rinsed and drained
2 cups tomato juice
2 tbs. brown sugar

Remove and discard core from cabbage. Place cabbage in boiling water to cover, and cook for about 6 minutes. Remove from water and cool. Spray a large sauté pan with nonstick cooking spray and cook chopped onions, garlic, leeks and bacon over medium-high heat. Sauté only until vegetables are wilted and slightly brown. Remove from pan and add chopped tomatoes and parsley. In a separate pan, sauté ground meats until no longer pink. Remove from heat and add ½ of the onion mixture, rice, cinnamon, nutmeg, salt and pepper.

Remove leaves carefully from cabbage. Trim center ribs to facilitate rolling. (If cabbage leaves are not pliable enough, return to boiling water for 1 to 2 minutes). Heat oven to 400°. Place about ¼ cup of the meat mixture in the center of each cabbage leaf, turn sides in, and roll up. Repeat with remaining leaves. Chop any remaining cabbage and mix with sauerkraut. Spray a heavy 4-quart casserole with nonstick cooking spray. Sprinkle some of the onion mixture and some of the sauerkraut mixture on bottom of pot. Place filled cabbage rolls on top, fitting them snugly. Cover with another layer of onion mixture and sauerkraut mixture, and more cabbage rolls. Repeat, ending with a layer of vegetables. Pour tomato juice over all and sprinkle with brown sugar. Place a layer of parchment paper on top to help contain juices. Cover tightly, and bake for 20 minutes. Reduce heat to 350° and bake for 2½ hours until tender.

GUMBO AND RICE

This is an adaptation of a recipe concocted by a friend whose love of spicy food is very evident here. Keep tasting and testing when preparing this recipe. Much depends on one's individual hot spice-meter.

4 cups chicken stock (see page 17)
10 cups water
1 bottle Cajun King gumbo mix or Louisiana Cajun Meat Magic
10 small red potatoes, unpeeled, cut into eighths
3 stalks celery, diced
1 large white onion, diced
1 tbs. tomato paste
3 whole heads garlic, peeled and finely chopped
5 strips bacon, cooked, fat reserved
1 lb. smoked sausage, cut into ½-inch slices
2 lb. chicken breasts and thighs, boned, cut into 1½-inch pieces

vegetable oil, if needed
8-12 cloves garlic, minced
1 medium onion, diced
1 tbs. vegetable oil
1 pkg. (10 oz.) frozen okra
cracked black pepper to taste
1 can (14 oz.) stewed tomatoes
1 green bell pepper, chopped
2 bunches scallions, white and green parts, chopped
Jane's Crazy Mixed Up Pepper or Lawry's Seasoned Pepper to taste
6 cups medium-grain cooked white rice (see page 10)

In a 6-quart pot, bring chicken stock, water and Cajun King gumbo mix to a boil; reduce heat and simmer for about 15 minutes. Add potatoes, celery, large onion, tomato paste and 3 heads chopped garlic to stock. Keep mixture at a simmer. Crumble bacon and set aside. Sauté smoked sausage in bacon fat over medium-high heat until browned. Remove sausage, reserving bacon fat. Sauté chicken meat in remaining bacon fat over medium-high heat until cooked. Add vegetable oil if necessary. Return bacon and sausage to pan, combine with chicken and set aside.

In another large skillet, sauté 8-12 cloves minced garlic and medium onion in 1 tbs. vegetable oil. Add okra and sauté for 3 to 4 minutes. Add cracked black pepper to taste. Drain stewed tomatoes and add to okra mixture. Cook for 5 minutes. Add sausage-bacon-chicken mixture and okra mixture to simmering stock mixture. Add green pepper, scallions and Jane's Crazy Mixed Up Pepper. Simmer for 4 hours or more. The amount should be reduced by about 1/3. Pour into soup bowls and pass hot rice.

JAMBALAYA

Jambalaya is the legitimate descendant of Spanish paella. New Orleans is its birthplace, and since its genes are fiery, you may decide to temper it to your own taste. I prefer the heat of this recipe just as it is. A cold beer and soothing salad go well with this dish.

3 tbs. vegetable oil
½ lb. lean smoked ham, diced
½ lb. fatback or slab bacon, cut into ½-inch dice
1 lb. smoked sausage, cut in half lengthwise and sliced
1 green bell pepper, chopped
3 large sweet onions, peeled and chopped
6 cloves garlic, minced
½ cup chopped fresh flat-leaf parsley
1 dried hot red chile pepper, seeded and crushed
1 tsp. dried thyme

1 tsp. dried oregano
1 tsp. freshly ground black pepper, or more to taste
¼ tsp. cayenne pepper, or more to taste
½ tbs. salt, or more to taste
1 lb. chicken breast, boned and skinned
¼ cup flour
2 cups long-grain white rice
4 cups simmering chicken stock, or half chicken and half fish stock (see page 17, 16)
1 lb. peeled, deveined large shrimp
1 lb. shucked oysters, optional

Heat oil in a heavy, 8-quart pot over medium-high heat. Add ham, fatback and sausage. Sauté until light brown. Add pepper, onions, garlic and parsley and sauté until slightly wilted. Add crushed red pepper, thyme, oregano, black and cayenne peppers and salt. Stir for 1 or 2 minutes. Dredge chicken with flour and sauté briefly in the same pan. Add rice and stir to coat all grains with oil and vegetables. Add stock, reserving ½ cup, bring to a boil briefly, cover with a tight-fitting lid and lower heat. Cook for about 45 minutes, checking every 6 or 8 minutes to make sure liquid has not boiled off; if dry, add reserved stock. About 10 minutes before dish is done, taste for seasoning. Add more cayenne, black pepper or salt if desired. Blend additions carefully and cover. Add peeled shrimp and oysters for the last 5 minutes of cooking.

VARIATION
Change the character of this dish by making it all seafood, or no seafood. Add 1 tsp. chili powder with the other dried spices.

LAMB AND RISOTTO PIE

This is a wonderful way to use leftover roast lamb. It has been so popular with friends and family that I sometimes make it using freshly ground lamb, which provides the same blending of flavors that seems to satisfy that need for a home-cooked taste. The cumin, curry powder and mint are tasty additions.

3 tbs. olive oil
3 leeks, white part only, cleaned and
  diced
1 medium onion, minced
3 cloves garlic, minced
2 tbs. cumin seeds, toasted and ground
  (see page 9)
1 tbs. curry powder
2 cups Arborio rice
5 cups hot beef stock (see page 18)
4 oz. crumbled feta cheese
½ cup chopped fresh mint or basil

6 cups diced cooked lamb
1 small jalapeño pepper, seeded and
  finely diced
1 red bell pepper, diced
1 tbs. hot sauce, such as Tabasco
1 cup drained canned Italian tomatoes,
  chopped
1 tsp. salt
¼ tsp. freshly ground pepper
2 tbs. butter

Heat olive oil in an uncovered pressure cooker over medium heat. Sauté leeks, onions and garlic until soft. Add cumin and curry. Cook briefly. Add Arborio rice and turn to coat all grains with oil. Add hot stock. Place lid on pot and bring to high pressure. Cook for 10 minutes. Remove from heat, reduce pressure and remove lid. The rice will not be fully cooked. Mix in feta cheese and chopped fresh mint or basil. Heat oven to 350°. Combine cooked lamb with jalapeño pepper, red bell pepper, hot sauce, tomatoes, salt and pepper. In a medium sauté pan, sauté for 5 minutes over medium heat. Remove from heat. Spoon into a shallow 3-quart baking dish. Spread risotto evenly over top. Dot with 2 tbs. butter. Bake for 25 to 30 minutes, until rice is slightly brown and crusty.

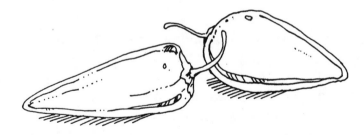

LAMB CURRY WITH BROWN RICE

Servings: 6

It is difficult to think of a word other than "leftover" that describes food remaining at the end of a meal that is still good, but needs to be resuscitated in some way that is pleasing to the palate. An old friend of mine uses the term "encore."

1 cup brown rice
¼ tsp. salt
2½ cups chicken stock (see page 17) or water
¾ cup chopped onions
3 cloves garlic, minced
1 cup chopped seeded, peeled tomatoes, pureed

2 tbs. tomato paste, or more
½ tsp. red pepper flakes, or more to taste
1 tsp. curry powder
½-1 cup boiling water
3 cups cooked lamb, chicken or beef, cut into bite-sized pieces

Bring rice, salt and chicken stock to a boil in a heavy 1-quart pot with a tight-fitting lid. Cover and reduce heat. Simmer for 30 to 40 minutes. Turn off heat and steam for 20 minutes. Fluff with a fork before serving. Spray a sauté pan with nonstick cooking spray. While rice is cooking, sauté onion and garlic over medium heat until onions are translucent. Add tomatoes, tomato paste, red pepper flakes, curry powder and water. Simmer until thickened, about 10 to 15 minutes, stirring occasionally. Add meat and stir over low heat for 5 minutes. Serve over cooked brown rice.

KOREAN SPICY RICE

Servings: 4

This is a very spicy dish. Adjust the chili powder to suit your palate. A cool cucumber and yogurt salad makes a good accompaniment.

3 tbs. vegetable oil
12 oz. lean pork loin, finely diced
3 cloves garlic, minced
1 tbs. grated ginger root
2 tsp. ground dried red chile pepper
1½ cups thinly sliced scallions, white
    and green parts

4 cups chicken stock
4 tbs. soy sauce
2 tbs. rice vinegar
2 cups long-grain rice
1 tsp. salt

Heat oil in a small skillet over medium heat and add diced pork. Cook until no longer pink. Add garlic and ginger, and sauté for 1 to 2 minutes. Add ground chile pepper and scallions. Stir mixture and heat for 3 to 4 minutes. Remove ½ of the mixture and set aside. Transfer remaining pork mixture to a 2-quart pot with a tight-fitting lid. Add chicken stock, soy sauce, vinegar, rice and salt. Bring to a boil, reduce heat and cover. Simmer for 20 minutes. Remove from heat and keep covered for 5 to 10 minutes. Mix in reserved pork mixture, cover and allow flavors to blend for 5 to 10 minutes. Serve hot.

MALAYAN RICE AND PORK

Servings: 6

If the thick sweet soy sauce in this recipe is difficult to find, you can add 1 tbs. dark molasses to regular soy sauce. The sweetness in the sauce helps in caramelizing the pork, and adds an exotic authenticity to the dish. Lemon grass can be found both dried and fresh in specialty stores and in some supermarkets, as is glutinous rice, which is somewhat sticky. You can use regular long-grain rice, cooked according to package directions.

RICE
2 cups glutinous rice
6 cups water
½ tsp. turmeric
1 tbs. chopped dried lemon grass

3 bay leaves
1 cup canned light coconut milk
1 cup water
salt to taste

TOPPING
1 lb. pork loin, diced
1 onion, thinly sliced
3 cloves garlic, minced
2 tbs. vegetable oil
1 tbs. ground ginger

¼ cup sweet thick soy sauce
¾ cup water
2 tbs. sugar
3 scallions, chopped

At least 6 hours before cooking rice, rinse in several changes of cold water until water runs clear. Soak rice for 6 to 12 hours in 6 cups water. Combine turmeric, lemon grass, bay leaves, coconut milk and 1 cup water in a 6-cup pot (preferably the top of a double boiler) and add rice. Directly over heat, bring to a boil, and reduce heat immediately. Cover and cook for 10 minutes only. Place pot over simmering water, and steam for 20 to 30 minutes. Add salt, if necessary. Fluff with a fork and serve.

For topping, sauté pork, onion and garlic in oil over medium-high heat until light brown. Add ginger and sauté for 1 to 2 minutes. Combine soy sauce, water and sugar and add to mixture. Simmer for about 10 minutes. Sprinkle with scallions and mix briefly. Serve hot or at room temperature over rice.

PORK LOIN ROLLS WITH TOMATO MADEIRA SAUCE

Servings: 6

Thinly sliced boneless pork loin, stuffed with sun-dried tomatoes and rice, is briefly cooked and served with a creamy tomato wine sauce. It's a perfect menu choice for a company dinner, as it can be fully prepared and reheated in the microwave without loss of texture or flavor. Besides that, it tastes great! Broiled tomatoes and buttered string beans would go well with this entrée.

2 tbs. olive oil
½ cup minced onion
1 clove garlic, minced
1 tbs. dried rosemary
½ tsp. salt
freshly ground pepper to taste
3 tbs. finely chopped fresh rosemary
1 cup chopped sun-dried tomatoes
4 cups cooked risotto (see pages 13-23)
12-18 thin slices pork loin, about
    1-2 oz. each

1 clove garlic, halved
salt and freshly ground pepper to taste
1 cup flour
2 tbs. butter
2 tbs. olive oil
2 tbs. tomato paste
1 cup chicken stock (see page 17)
1 cup heavy cream
½ cup dry or medium-dry Madeira wine

Heat oven to 300°. Heat olive oil in a large heavy sauté pan. Add onion, garlic and dried rosemary and sauté until onion is soft, and not brown. Add salt, pepper and fresh rosemary. Remove from heat and combine mixture with sun-dried tomatoes and cooked risotto. Place pork loin between 2 pieces plastic wrap and pound until about 1/4-inch thick. Rub both sides with the cut side of garlic clove and sprinkle with salt and pepper. Place 1/3 cup of the rice filling on one side of each piece of pork and roll into a cylindrical shape. Tie with kitchen string, or secure with bamboo skewers or toothpicks.

Dredge each roll with flour. Heat butter and oil in a medium sauté pan. Over high heat, sear 2 or 3 pork rolls on all sides. Do not crowd pan. Remove rolls as they are seared, and keep warm in the oven, covered lightly with foil, while preparing sauce. When all rolls have been seared, scrape any brown pieces loose from bottom of pan with a wooden spoon and add tomato paste. Continue stirring and add chicken stock. When stock is reduced by half, add cream and Madeira. Reduce heat and simmer sauce until reduced and thickened. Strain and set aside. Serve 2 or 3 pork rolls per person, and ladle sauce over each serving.

BUFFET TURKEY TONNATO RISOTTO

This is a palate-pleasing entrée to complement any buffet. Arrange the turkey slices on highly seasoned cold risotto and top it with a pungent tonnato (tuna) sauce.

6 cups cooked risotto (see pages 13-23)
3 tbs. grated fresh lemon peel (zest)
1/4 cup chopped kalamata olives
6-8 cloves garlic, minced
6 tbs. chopped fresh cilantro
1/2 cup *Vinaigrette* (see page 95) mixed
    with 1 additional tbs. Dijon mustard
3/4 cup drained capers
8 cans (63/4 oz. each) flaked tuna,
    drained
2 1/2 cups olive oil, or 1 cup olive oil and
    1 cup chicken stock

3 cans (2 oz. each) anchovy fillets, with
    oil
1/3 cup lemon juice
1 tsp. salt
freshly ground pepper to taste
20 red leaf lettuce leaves
5-7 lb. cooked turkey breast, cut into
    1/4-inch slices
fresh cilantro leaves for garnish
lemon slices for garnish

Combine cooked risotto with lemon peel, olives, ½ of the minced garlic, and cilantro. Add ½ cup mustard *Vinaigrette* and mix lightly to blend. Add ½ cup capers, mixing lightly so rice grains do not become mushy. Place drained tuna in a food processor workbowl with remaining minced garlic. Turn on the motor and add olive oil slowly to form a thick emulsion. Leave motor running and add anchovies. Add lemon juice. Stop motor and test for seasonings. Add salt and pepper if desired.

Arrange 20 lettuce leaves, not overlapping, on a large serving platter. Place a mound of rice mixture, about ⅓ to ½ cup, on each lettuce leaf. Place a slice of turkey breast on top of each mound of rice. Spread some tuna sauce over turkey, enough to cover mound entirely. Garnish with remaining capers, lemon slices and cilantro. Serve extra sauce in a separate bowl.

RISOTTO CHICKEN PACKETS

Servings: 8

This dish works very well for a large crowd, since it can be prepared ahead of time. Each serving is individually wrapped, and as it is cut open at the table, it provides an aroma and cachet that is unbeatable. The creaminess of the risotto holds everything together. These packets can be prepared ahead of time, and kept refrigerated until baking. You can use other vegetables instead, such as sliced broccoli, asparagus or roasted red peppers.

½ cup diced shallots
¼ cup butter
1 tbs. dried tarragon, or ½ cup
    chopped fresh
5 tbs. flour
4 cups chicken stock (see page 17)
¾ cup dry white wine
2 cups heavy cream
2 cups toasted almonds, ground (see
    page 8)
1¾ cups stone-ground Dijon mustard

salt and freshly ground pepper to taste
2 lb. chicken breast, boned, cut into
    1-inch strips
½ lb. string beans, trimmed
3 large carrots, cut into thin matchstick
    strips, blanched
2 large leeks, cleaned, white and pale
    green parts sliced into thin rounds
4 cups cooked risotto (see pages 13-
    23)

Heat oven to 375°. Sauté shallots in butter over medium heat until soft. Add tarragon and sauté for 3 to 4 minutes. Add flour and stir thoroughly. If it is too thick, add a small amount of the chicken stock. When flour, butter and shallots are well combined, add chicken stock slowly, whisking continuously. Add white wine and cream, and simmer until reduced by ⅓. Remove from heat and cool. Mix ground almonds and mustard into cooled sauce and taste for seasonings. Add salt and pepper if needed. Increase oven temperature to 375°.

Make 8 packets: For each, begin with a rectangle of parchment paper or aluminum foil about 16-x-20 inches. Fold in half lengthwise. Cut half a heart shape from paper or foil; when opened, fold will be in the center of heart. On half of paper, spoon some almond mustard sauce. On sauce, lay about 5 strips of the chicken. Layer with some beans, some carrot strips and sliced leeks. Add ½ cup of the cooked risotto. Add another layer of sauce. Try to keep edges of paper clean. Fold one side of the heart over contents, and crimp edges to seal paper tightly, beginning at the rounded curve. Place packets on a baking sheet and bake for 20 to 25 minutes. Serve immediately to take advantage of the dramatic-looking puffy shape. Each diner should have a sharp knife to slit packet.

STUFFED CHICKEN BREASTS ALMONDINE

Almost every culture with rice in its culinary tradition has a unique approach to a filling for chicken breasts. One thing in common is that almost all of the dishes can be served hot or cold. In this recipe, the assertive flavor of the savory brown rice is softened by almonds and tarragon. You can substitute low-fat milk for the beaten eggs. This entrée can be prepared well in advance.

8 chicken breast halves, skinned and boned, trimmed of fat
1/2 cup finely chopped onions
2 cloves garlic, minced
2 tbs. olive oil
1/4 cup chopped fresh tarragon, or 2 tbs. dried
1 cup cooked brown rice (see page 10)
1 1/2 cups blanched sliced almonds, toasted (see page 8)
salt and freshly ground pepper to taste
1 cup all-purpose flour
2 eggs, beaten with 1/4 cup water
1 cup fine breadcrumbs
1 cup ground almonds
1/4 cup butter, melted, or 2 tbs. melted butter and 2 tbs. olive oil

Line a baking sheet with buttered parchment paper or aluminum foil. Place chicken breast halves between pieces of waxed paper and pound until almost transparent. Sauté onions and garlic in 2 tbs. oil over medium heat until soft. Add dried tarragon, if using, and sauté briefly. Combine onion and garlic mixture, rice, almonds and fresh tarragon, if using, and mix well. Lay chicken breasts on a flat surface. Sprinkle with salt and pepper. Place a generous ¼ cup of the filling on each breast. Fold sides in toward center and roll up breast. Dip filled breast in flour and then in beaten egg mixture. Mix breadcrumbs and ground almonds together. Roll breasts in crumbs and place 2 inches apart on prepared baking sheet. Chill for 30 minutes.

Heat oven to 400°. Roast stuffed breasts for 20 to 25 minutes, brushing once or twice with melted butter. Serve hot or at room temperature.

VARIATION

Cut at an angle into ¼-inch slices and serve as an hors d'oeuvre accompanied by a sauce of your choice, such as Aioli.

SUNDAY BEEF AND RICE POT ROAST

Servings: 6

The aroma of a slow-cooking pot roast in the oven reminds me of earlier days when Sundays meant that the family would dine together, and the meal would be eaten leisurely. A late afternoon meal meant that foraging for supper would be left up to the individual, and it would most likely be leftover pot roast and gravy poured over whatever available carbohydrate was around. But the first go-around was marvelous with plain white long-grain rice cooked with additional aromatics in the same pot.

2 tbs. vegetable oil
3 medium carrots, cut into half-rounds
1 large Spanish onion, peeled and coarsely diced
4 large cloves garlic, chopped
3-4 lb. boneless beef chuck roast, fat trimmed
2 cloves garlic, minced
1 tsp. salt
1 tbs. freshly ground pepper

½ cup flour
1 large can (28 oz.) whole peeled tomatoes, with juice
½ leek, white part only, finely diced
1 large shallot, peeled and diced
1 tbs. vegetable oil
1 tbs. dried basil, or 3 tbs. chopped fresh
2 cups long-grain white rice

Heat oven to 300°. On the stovetop over medium-high heat, heat 2 tbs. oil in a large ovenproof pot that has a tight-fitting lid. Add carrots, onion and chopped garlic and sauté until slightly brown. Remove from pot. Rub meat with minced garlic, salt and pepper on all sides. Rub flour well into meat. If pot appears to be too dry, spray it with nonstick cooking spray. When pot is very hot, sear meat over high heat for at least 5 minutes on each side. Remove pot from heat. Return vegetables to pot and add tomatoes with juice. Cover and cook in oven for at least 3 hours. Do not allow liquid to boil; lower heat, if necessary, to maintain a simmer. When meat is fork-tender, remove from oven. In a skillet over medium heat, sauté leek and shallots in 1 tbs. vegetable oil. Add basil and sauté for 1 minute. Stir leek mixture and rice into contents of pot. Cover and return to oven for 45 minutes.

VEAL ORLOFF GRATIN

Servings: 6-8

This is a greatly simplified version of a classic French veal entrée. Chunks of veal are braised and covered by a thick sauce made with onions, mushrooms and rice topped with grated Gruyère cheese. Yes, it's pretty rich. Save it for a special occasion, and you won't feel deprived when you watch your diet the rest of the time.

3 lb. veal shoulder, fat and cartilage trimmed, cut into 2-inch chunks
salt and freshly ground pepper to taste
2 tbs. minced garlic
2 tbs. all-purpose or superfine flour
1/4 cup olive oil
2 tbs. Madeira wine, optional

1/2 cup chicken or beef stock (see page 17, 18)
8 oz. white mushrooms
Sauce Soubise, follows
1 cup cooked long-grain rice (see page 10), optional
3 tbs. grated Gruyère cheese

Heat oven to 350°. Place veal chunks in a bowl with salt, pepper, garlic and flour. Toss to coat evenly. Heat 2 tbs. of the olive oil in a large ovenproof skillet or Dutch oven. Sear veal, a few pieces at a time. Do not crowd pan. Remove each piece after it is browned on all sides. When all meat is browned, add Madeira to pan, if using, and stock. Scrape browned bits from bottom of pan. Remove pan from heat and set aside.

If mushroom caps are very large, cut into quarters. In another skillet, heat remaining 2 tbs. oil. Sauté mushrooms over high heat for about 5 minutes, until brown. Add mushrooms, *Sauce Soubise* and cooked rice, if using, to veal. Return mixture to original skillet and bake for about 45 minutes. Remove from oven, sprinkle with grated Gruyère cheese and return to oven until cheese is bubbling.

SAUCE SOUBISE

This makes a spectacular sauce for lamb or veal, and can also be used as a filling for vegetables. In that case, do not strain, but use the entire mixture.

2 large sweet onions
6 tbs. unsalted butter
2 cups cooked risotto (see pages 13-23)
1 cup heavy cream

1 tsp. lemon juice
freshly ground white pepper to taste
½ tsp. salt

Slice onions very thinly, or process with a food processor. Be careful not to overprocess, as they will turn bitter. Melt butter in a heavy sauté pan over medium-low heat and sauté onions until golden, but not brown, about 25 minutes. This may be facilitated by covering the pan and lowering the heat. Add rice, mix lightly, cover and heat for 5 minutes. Add cream and cook for 1 to 2 minutes. Remove from heat, cool slightly, process to a fine puree and strain. Season with lemon juice, white pepper and salt. Taste for seasonings and adjust if necessary.

CREAMY MUSHROOM RISOTTO CASSEROLE
Servings: 6-8

This vegetarian recipe is delectable and satisfying. Vegetable or chicken stock adds punch to the flavor of the slowly simmered mushrooms and onions.

1/2 cup butter
3 cups sliced sweet onions
1 cup vegetable or chicken stock (see page 15, 17)
2 tbs. flour

pinch nutmeg
1 lb. white mushrooms, thinly sliced
1/2 cup heavy cream
4 cups cooked risotto (see pages 13-23)

Heat oven to 350°. Melt 1/2 of the butter in a heavy sauté pan over medium heat and add sliced onions. Sauté onions until soft. Do not brown. Add vegetable or chicken stock. Cover pan and reduce heat to low. Cook for 15 to 20 minutes, checking occasionally. Add flour and nutmeg and stir until flour is dissolved. Heat remaining butter in another sauté pan over medium-high heat and add mushrooms. Sauté until brown. Drain mushrooms, reserving cooking liquid. Cook liquid until reduced by half. Add cooked mushrooms and reduced liquid to onions and mix well. Cook for 3 to 4 minutes. Stir in heavy cream. Combine risotto with onion-mushroom mixture and spoon into a 2 1/2- to 3-quart casserole. Bake for 20 to 30 minutes.

INDEX

Serve creative, easy, nutritious meals with nitty gritty® cookbooks

Wraps and Roll-Ups
Easy Vegetarian Cooking
Party Fare: Irresistible Nibbles
   for Every Occasion
Cappuccino/Espresso: The Book of
   Beverages
Fresh Vegetables
Cooking with Fresh Herbs
Cooking with Chile Peppers
The Dehydrator Cookbook
Recipes for the Pressure Cooker
Beer and Good Food
Unbeatable Chicken Recipes
Gourmet Gifts
From Freezer, 'Fridge and Pantry
Edible Pockets for Every Meal
Oven and Rotisserie Roasting
Risottos, Paellas and Other Rice
   Specialties
Muffins, Nut Breads and More
Healthy Snacks for Kids
100 Dynamite Desserts
Recipes for Yogurt Cheese
Sautés
Cooking in Porcelain

Casseroles
The Toaster Oven Cookbook
Skewer Cooking on the Grill
Creative Mexican Cooking
Marinades
No Salt, No Sugar, No Fat Cookbook
Quick and Easy Pasta Recipes
Cooking in Clay
Deep Fried Indulgences
The Garlic Cookbook
From Your Ice Cream Maker
The Best Pizza is Made at Home
The Best Bagels are Made at Home
Convection Oven Cookery
The Steamer Cookbook
The Pasta Machine Cookbook
The Versatile Rice Cooker
The Bread Machine Cookbook
The Bread Machine Cookbook II
The Bread Machine Cookbook III
The Bread Machine Cookbook IV:
   Whole Grains & Natural Sugars
The Bread Machine Cookbook V:
   *Favorite Recipes from 100
   Kitchens*

The Bread Machine Cookbook VI:
   *Hand-Shaped Breads from the
   Dough Cycle*
Worldwide Sourdoughs from Your
   Bread Machine
Entrées from Your Bread Machine
The New Blender Book
The Sandwich Maker Cookbook
Waffles
The Coffee Book
The Juicer Book I and II
Bread Baking
The 9 x 13 Pan Cookbook
Recipes for the Loaf Pan
Low Fat American Favorites
Healthy Cooking on the Run
Favorite Seafood Recipes
New International Fondue Cookbook
Favorite Cookie Recipes
Cooking for 1 or 2
The Well Dressed Potato
Extra-Special Crockery Pot Recipes
Slow Cooking
The Wok

For a free catalog, write or call: Bristol Publishing Enterprises, Inc.
P.O. Box 1737, San Leandro, CA 94577 (800) 346-4889